Against My Better Judgement

Terry Maher founded Pentos in 1972 and was chairman and chief executive until 1993. He was responsible for building Dillons Bookstores into Britain's largest specialist bookseller and for establishing new retail standards in the book trade. He is married with three grown-up sons and lives in London and the Cotswolds.

Against My Better Judgement

Adventures in the City
and in the Book Trade

TERRY MAHER

Mandarin

To all who have worked at Pentos

A Mandarin Paperback
AGAINST MY BETTER JUDGEMENT

First published in Great Britain 1994
by Sinclair-Stevenson
This edition published 1995
by Mandarin Paperbacks
an imprint of Reed International Books Ltd
Michelin House, 81 Fulham Road, London SW3 6RB
and Auckland, Melbourne, Singapore and Toronto

A CIP catalogue record for this title
is available from the British Library
ISBN 0 7493 2152 0

Printed and bound in Great Britain
by Cox & Wyman Ltd, Reading, Berkshire

Contents

It must be considered that there is nothing more difficult to carry out, nor more doubtful of success, nor more dangerous to handle, than to initiate a new order of things. For the reformer has enemies in all those who profit by the old order and only lukewarm defenders in all those who would profit by the new.

Machiavelli – *The Prince*

He that filches from me my good name
Robs me of that which not enriches him
And makes me poor indeed

Shakespeare – *Othello*

1

Pentos Takes Off

We were meeting in the offices of the stockbrokers Kitcat and Aitken, in January 1972, to form a new company. I had been working in London since May 1969 with First National Finance Corporation, latterly as a main board director. At FNFC I was responsible for its investment banking activities and I had become particularly identified with two public companies in which FNFC had a large shareholding. When the original investment had been made, they were both small companies, with indifferent records and poor management. They were what the City termed 'special situations'; companies where some change of management or direction was expected and where normal investment valuation criteria did not apply. There could be rich pickings – or the company could go bust. One, the Austin Hall Group, was mainly involved in the manufacture of joinery and garden sheds and greenhouses. The other, Marshall Morgan and Scott, was involved in publishing religious books and a newspaper titled *The Life of Faith*. I had joined the boards of both companies to represent FNFC's interest. I had assumed a position of some influence and become recognised in the City as the architect of their fortunes, which were now very much in the ascendant. The share prices had responded accordingly.

The chief executive of FNFC was its entrepreneurial founder Pat Matthews. He and I were now in disagreement and it had therefore been decided that I would leave to pursue 'other interests'. I was to seek to place with institutions half of FNFC's shareholdings in the two companies. At the same time I was to enter into service contracts with each of them and to purchase some of the shares myself. These acts of confidence, it was thought, would make it more likely that the institutions would take the shares which were to be offered to them. FNFC would make a large profit on its investment and would still retain half its holding. For me it was an important opportunity but also a major commitment. I had borrowed £200,000 from Barclays Bank and purchased shares from FNFC which had a market value of £250,000. The difference of £50,000 was effectively a fee for placing FNFC's shares. But I was very seriously at risk, because, as we are told incessantly, shares can go down as well as up – and, as I had no money of my own, the consequences of failure would have been disastrous even if I did not fully appreciate it at the time. All of this was happening very quickly and I was advised that for tax and other reasons I should form a company to hold my shares rather than holding them personally. My solicitors said they would supply the company off the shelf. It was a 'shell' company with £100 issued share capital named Pentos. They explained that a change could be made to a more appropriate name at a later date. The meeting in Kitcat and Aitken's offices was to finalise the documentation and to brief its salesmen so that they could market the shares in Austin Hall and Marshall Morgan and Scott to the investing institutions. The placing was quickly achieved and a press release announced the news, including the purchase of the shares by Pentos; and it was stated rather grandly that this £100 fledgling would also be seeking to make further investments in other areas of activity. There were to be many more press releases in the next twenty tumultuous, roller-coaster years, but none has been more significant.

It had never remotely occurred to me that I might one day start my own business. I was born in Viaduct Street in one of the poorer parts of Manchester on December 5, 1935. My father came from a large Catholic family whose Irish origins were two generations earlier. They were respectable working class with strong women and weak men. My mother's family were virulently anti-Catholic Protestants and her marriage made her for a while something of an outcast within her own family and consequently her life very difficult. It is impossible to exaggerate today how bitter the divisions were between Catholic and Protestant families at that time. My parents were married in a Catholic church and I was brought up a Catholic and went to Catholic schools. My father worked in the newspaper industry in Manchester as a member of the infamous NATSOPA trades union and he was relatively well paid for unskilled, undemanding work. Unfortunately, the prevailing culture in that part of the newspaper world meant that much of the money did not find its way home and it was therefore far from plentiful. However, we were never without food and clothes, although the two-up and two-down houses with leaking roofs and freezing outside lavatories left a lot to be desired. An early luxury was my first pair of new wooden clogs which meant that I could then compete in 'kicking' sparks. The clogs were shod with metal runners which threw up sparks from hard contact with the cobbled street. An early memory was of the street dawn patrol by the 'knockers-up'. These were paid pennies a week by each household so that with their long sticks they would rattle the bedroom window from the street at an agreed hour to ensure that the bread-winner got to the local cotton mill or factory on time. Alarm clocks were still a long way off.

I attended St Anne's School in Ancoats from where I won a scholarship to Xaverian College. My mother was not to hear the news. She had suffered a long illness throughout most of my childhood and she died three months before the letter arrived. I was eleven and she was thirty-four. My father was devastated and never fully recovered. For the next dozen years we (my father, my younger brother and I) lived mainly with his mother, my grandmother, although my father would have spells of independence, usually after a quarrel, when we took off to live in a home of our own; I would then find that I had to assume the role of housekeeper for the three of us. My grandmother was a remarkable woman: strong, frugal and wise. She brought up eight of her own children and at different times many of her grandchildren. She saw enormous sadness but was invariably cheerful. She made sure that I always had a home. My father lived an aimless, unhappy life for the thirty years after my mother's death and did not re-marry. He did, however, in his later years, take a great and proud interest in the development of my career.

Xaverian College was probably the best Catholic grammar school in Manchester. It was a Jesuitical education and most of the teaching staff belonged to the order of

St Francis Xavier. They were presided over by the headmaster, Brother Martin, a formidable, stern disciplinarian. Many years later I was to meet one of my idols, Anthony Burgess, at lunch and I said to him that we were both at Xaverian College – although not at the same time; 'Brother Martin' was his immediate reaction as he slapped his thigh. Brother Martin was not a person whom one ever forgot.

In the first term at Xaverian I settled down surprisingly quickly. In the end-of-term examinations I was placed third in my form, but it was explained to me that the two boys ahead of me were not from the new intake and therefore had an unfair advantage. I would never do so well at school again. In the middle of the second term I contracted tuberculosis and spent a year in a sanatorium. I never made up for that lost time and my subsequent years at Xaverian were a disappointment to me and to my teachers. I found it difficult to sustain the hard work and dedicated enthusiasm which would have been required to catch up. I left at sixteen with a sense of missed opportunity. Within a year I was back in hospital. The tuberculosis had recurred and I lost a further year in a sanatorium before returning to what the doctor told me could never be a normal life. I was not immediately able to look for work as I was still under medical supervision and had to attend hospital for treatment each week. I soon tired of this useless existence and obtained part-time work in an accountant's office. At the time I did not know what an accountant did – school careers guidance was then almost non-existent. I found the work undemanding and persuaded my doctor to allow me to take up full-time employment. At the same time I started to study from home to take the accountancy examinations. I worked hard in my spare time for the intermediate examination and was rewarded by a prize, being placed third in the overall order of merit. I did less well in the finals, as by then I had developed new interests which proved distracting. I had married and had also become actively involved in politics. Academic study had become a burden.

I was twenty-four when, in 1960, I qualified. I went to work for an American abrasives manufacturer, Carborundum, in Trafford Park in Manchester, to gain commercial experience. I stayed for eight years. It was a satisfying time. I gained experience of every aspect of a basic manufacturing business with an important research and development function and with markets throughout the world. Accountancy took on a new dimension as I was able to use it as an aid to making business decisions. I tried to demystify accounting and to make it more understandable to my non-accounting colleagues. I also devised a series of incentive plans for each unit within the business which at the time was considered fairly revolutionary. It led to a major feature in the *Financial Times* – an early experience of the national press. My ideas on incentive plans, and on a more practical approach to the use of accounting techniques, meant that I was asked to speak at a number of management courses at the University in Manchester and at management seminars in Brussels. Carborundum's American ownership and international business also meant that I frequently travelled to America and to Europe. My horizons were widened considerably and my self-confidence was boosted. When I left Carborundum I was head of finance in their European operations and number three in their overall hierarchy. But, at the age of thirty-three, it was time for me to move on. My lectures in Brussels had brought me to the attention of headhunters and I was persuaded in 1969 to relocate to London.

In preparation for my accountancy examinations, I was required to study economics. I found it to be far from dull, and I began to read more widely on the subject and to take the *Economist* magazine each week. My grandmother used to confuse the local newsagent, and embarrass me, by always referring to it as the *Communist*. I read the *Economist* from the age of twenty until only two or three years ago, when it was replaced by the *Spectator*. In those early years the *Economist* was a more serious academic journal covering UK economic and political issues in great detail in a dry but, I thought, very readable style. My interest in economics had extended naturally into politics and my other regular reading at that time was the *Manchester Guardian*.

In 1956, Britain's Conservative Government, under the leadership of Anthony Eden, became involved in the ill-fated 'Suez Crisis'. The Egyptian leader Colonel Nasser had nationalised the Suez Canal in July 1956 and Anglo-French forces invaded Egypt in October on the pretext of separating Egyptian and Israeli troops who were already in conflict. It was clear, however, that there had been collusion between the British, French and Israelis, and that the real purpose of the invasion was to re-take the canal. There was world-wide condemnation, not least from the United Nations and the United States. The whole enterprise was a fiasco, ended in ignominious withdrawal, and was deeply damaging to British interests. Political passions in this country, however, were raised in a manner rarely seen before or since. Members of families were turned against each other. In some quarters it was thought treasonable to question any aspect of the 'adventure'. The Labour Party supported the Government in the early stages but later relented. The Liberal Party stood out in unequivocal condemnation. In the media, the *Manchester Guardian* took a similar position. This proved to be very unpopular and cost it precious circulation – but it never faltered in its brave, honest and lonely stand. For me the Suez Crisis was a catalyst – I had to be involved in politics to seek to influence events, however remotely; and I was in no doubt that it was the Liberal Party in which I belonged. Jo Grimond had recently become leader and was articulating Liberal philosophy in a refreshingly relevant style. I wrote to the Manchester Liberal headquarters and asked to join the Party.

As there was no Liberal association in the council estate to which my grandmother had then moved, and in whose home I still lived, I was directed to Withington Young Liberals. I soon found that people who were prepared to take responsibility were few and far between. I quickly became an officer of the local association and then of the regional organisation. I met two like-minded young Liberals who were both to become good friends, Dennis Wrigley and Alan Share; the three of us would make an impact in Liberal politics in the North-West of England. We were vocal and energetic activists, often to the discomfort of the national organisation in London. We published jointly after the 1964 election two booklets, *Counterblast* (reviewed by Bertrand Russell) and *Effective Politics*, both of which received a wide circulation and which included a blunt message for Liberal Party headquarters that they should get their collective fingers out. We were not modest.

Apart from the regional political activity, I was elected to serve on the national committee of the League of Young Liberals. I had hardly ever been to London before I attended my first committee meeting and I was deeply suspicious of Southerners. Real people and real politics, I thought, resided in the North – and that mainly meant Manchester. I remember, on that first visit, a discussion over a sandwich lunch. Somebody was describing an experience whilst canvassing in a recent election in Kensington. Apparently an elector had said with some passion that she would not vote for the Conservative candidate because he split his infinitives. I was not entirely sure what a split infinitive might be; it was not a subject often raised on the doorsteps of Manchester. However, I have never forgotten that story and, as my recent colleagues will confirm, I have had a personal obsession with split infinitives ever since.

The purpose of political parties is to elect members of parliament; and, if I was serious in wanting to develop and pursue Liberal ideas and policies and to convert more people to my way of thinking, then I had to stand as a candidate. I was adopted as the prospective Liberal candidate for Accrington in January 1960. The recent general election had been held in October 1959 (Harold Macmillan and the Conservatives had been re-elected on the 'never had it so good' ticket) and I was therefore one of the first prospective candidates for the next election to be adopted and, at twenty-four, certainly the youngest.

Accrington was predominantly a working-class constituency represented by a Labour member of parliament but with a surprisingly resilient Conservative vote. It had not had a Liberal candidate for more than fifty years. There was only a skeleton Liberal organisation and very little money. For the next four years I worked with local Liberals in building up a ward organisation, fighting local elections and establishing a fund with which to fight the general election. I spent three nights each week in the constituency canvassing, visiting miners' clubs and other working men's clubs, attending committee meetings and addressing the occasional public meeting; a public meeting was often used as a way of starting a new local association. I also wrote a weekly column for the *Accrington Observer*. I would sit at home in front of my typewriter at two o'clock on a Sunday afternoon with the need to write 800 words on a subject of my choice (often still not decided) in time to meet the four o'clock deadline of the Sunday post.

The general election eventually came along in October 1964. There was a preliminary skirmish when the Conservatives changed their candidate at a late stage. It provided me with an opportunity for an early tilt at the establishment; there were to be more later. The new candidate was Victor Montagu, who had formerly been the Earl of Sandwich and who was married to a daughter of the Duke of Devonshire – a sister of the wife of Harold Macmillan. He had renounced his title under the enabling legislation which had recently been introduced as a result of a campaign by Tony Benn, formerly Viscount Stansgate. I made great play of the contrast between Mr Montagu's privileged background and the privations of many of his constituents. On news of his adoption I referred to him as an 'aristocratic anachronism', a remark which appeared on the front pages of a number of national newspapers.

The election campaign was hard work but enormous fun. Granada had just started TV broadcasts for all candidates in its area and we duly trooped before the cameras. Election meetings were well attended and we had a good reception on the doorstep. The opposition, we were told by the press, were getting just a little rattled. They need not have been. We polled respectably – saved our deposit, which was an achievement for a Liberal candidate at that time – but were a poor third. It had been an exhausting but exhilarating experience. The election had been decided on national issues and, as so often happens, the Liberal vote had been squeezed. It was the 'thirteen wasted years' election with the newly-appointed Conservative Prime Minister Sir Alec Douglas-Home, with his 'matchsticks' economics, seeking to defend his Party's record against Harold Wilson's promised 'white heat of the technological revolution'. Labour won but with an overall majority of only four and within two years there was the need for a further general election. This time I stood as the candidate for Runcorn in Cheshire. It was a constituency with better Liberal prospects and with a more middle-class electorate. We fought a more professional campaign with much better resources and we polled well. But I had preferred Accrington and its working men's clubs.

Shortly after the 1966 election, politics took a back seat for a while as I concentrated more on my career and the needs of a growing family. I had met Barbara in the Young Liberals in 1958. She was just about to finish her studies at Art College in Manchester and to take up a Gulbenkian scholarship at the British School in Rome. We married in 1960 and, by the time we made the move to London in 1969, we had three boys, Nicholas, Anthony and Jeremy. In my childhood home, books had been far from a feature of everyday life. My father thought it unnatural and unhealthy if he should see me reading indoors rather than out playing. Barbara's home was quite different. Her parents were cultured Jewish immigrants from Berlin. Barbara came to this country in her mother's arms in 1939. Her father had arrived just three months earlier. He was a remarkable man with great presence and personality who was to die at the tragically early age of fifty-eight. He was an eminent psychiatrist who had studied with Jung in Zurich and who had built a successful private practice in Manchester whilst also acting as a consultant at two local hospitals. Through Barbara my reading tastes and habits were to change. I was introduced to French classical literature, and read a little of the English classics to supplement the modest reading of my schooldays. I started to read contemporary fiction and biography, including political biography, and that taste has developed over the years so that it now contributes the major part of my reading. There remain, not surprisingly, enormous gaps in my knowledge of literature, but books became and remain an essential and important part in my life and few things have given me greater pleasure and satisfaction.

The decade of the 1960s had been a hectic time for me. I had developed a successful career at Carborundum; had been an energetic political activist, standing twice for parliament and several times in local elections, and publishing a wide range of articles, pamphlets and booklets; I had built a small accounting practice on my own which I ran from home; and I had tried to help Barbara bring up a demanding and growing family. I am afraid that, as so often happens, it was the family which took the strain. All of these interests were pursued in parallel in what sometimes seemed a frenzy of activity. I often reflected on the doctor who had told me fifteen years earlier that I would never be able to lead a normal life. Perhaps, in a way he had not intended, he was right. It was to be several years before I was quite so busy again. In May 1969 we moved to London.

The move from Manchester to London at the age of thirty-three was probably the most important single business decision I was ever to take. It was to change totally the prospects and fortunes of myself and my family. I had lived and worked in Manchester all of my life. I did not know London well, had visited it rarely, and had no knowledge whatsoever of its City and business areas. Having worked for an American company with its headquarters in Niagara Falls, I was more familiar with New York than with London.

The headhunters had introduced me to Pat Matthews. Pat had built a successful financial services group over a very short period of time; from a motor car hire purchase base, it had expanded rapidly into property (both as a principal and as a lender), and into stock market investment; it had also acquired an issuing house which could help small, new companies to obtain a stock market quotation. These were the heady go-go days of the swashbuckling late Sixties and early Seventies when Jim Slater was king. Pat Matthews, at the helm of First National Finance Corporation, was at the time only a minor baron in this domain but he was rising rapidly and he had pretensions. His ambition, which he was not quite to achieve, was to become one of the more respected merchant banking princes of the City of London.

Pat had enormous charisma and when he turned on the charm few could resist it; I was later to find that he could also be stubborn and determined. When I met him, I liked him straightaway and I had little hesitation in accepting the job which he offered to me at that first meeting. I was, initially, thrown just a little, as I had assumed that, with his name, his background was probably Irish Catholic, similar to my own; in fact he came from a family of East End Jewish cabinet makers – he had preferred the name of Pat to his given name of Percy. The job I was offered at FNFC contained two elements: to establish and assume responsibility for financial control within the rapidly growing group; and to set up and be responsible for a new subsidiary (to be called First National Holdings) which would make direct investments in businesses with turn-round potential and in which FNH would be able to exert an influence. I was to work closely with Pat in a top executive team of four or five people. It was the second element of the job description which was the main attraction, as the financial control role was one which I had already carried out on a wider scale.

I arrived in London on the first Sunday of May to be ready for work the following morning. Barbara and the boys (they were then aged eight, six and five) would join me some months later in a home we were to buy, with money borrowed from my new employer, in Hampstead Garden Suburb; in the meantime I was established in a flat in Marsham Court, a large apartment block, which FNFC had recently purchased with a view to selling off the individual units to its tenants. I walked out of the flat that sunny Sunday evening and strolled through the streets of Westminster and Victoria; I had been told that Jeremy Thorpe (then the leader of the Liberal Party) had an apartment in the same block, as did many other members of both Houses of Parliament, due to its convenient location; it seemed a long way from Manchester.

The first days at FNFC were very unsettling. I had been used to a structured organisation and an established routine; I had, at Carborundum, a number of managers reporting directly to me, and, most often, my working days were full, involved and satisfying; I was a very big fish in a fairly small pond. At FNFC, I was given an empty office, no secretary, no staff for whom I had direct responsibility; and no obvious duties. It was a totally new appointment and I was expected to flesh out the details around the skeleton of the bland job description and to create a real job with real responsibility and, most importantly, to establish some kind of authority. I quickly heard that there had been a number of other high-level appointments at FNFC over the past year or two and that they had rarely lasted more than two to three months; I felt that some of my new colleagues did not take me seriously because they were not sure that I would be around for very long. If, in those first few weeks, I had received a call from Carborundum asking me to go back, I have no doubt that I would have responded positively; it was one of the very few occasions in my business life when I suffered a loss of confidence and had doubts about my ability. However, I did not receive the half-hoped-for telephone call, therefore I had no alternative but to seek to establish a position for myself in which I could make a contribution to the fortunes of my new employer, exercise some influence over the future direction of the business, and work hard to win the confidence of my colleagues.

I introduced a system of financial control which established the returns on the financial assets which were the substance of FNFC's business and which measured their relative performance; I also improved existing systems so that risk was better identified and controlled (these systems were to be relaxed after my departure, with unfortunate consequences). I believed that these procedures were significantly ahead of those generally existing in finance houses and merchant banks in the City at that time. I settled into a satisfactory reporting relationship with the finance directors of the subsidiary companies but had a less easy relationship with the group finance director. One of the difficulties I had to overcome was the fact that on my arrival there was an existing group finance director who was to continue with that title although he had no responsibility for financial control. It was very much the way that Pat did things; he would appoint people with overlapping, if not conflicting, responsibilities and then leave them to sort themselves out.

My reputation at FNFC, however, was made primarily by the successful development of the investments in Austin Hall and Marshall Morgan and Scott. The stock market investment side of FNFC had purchased shares in the two companies in the hope of making things happen, but without any clear idea as to how to bring it about. I went along to talk to the respective directors of Austin Hall and Marshall Morgan and Scott and to persuade them that I had a role to play in helping them to develop their businesses; I joined their boards, eventually becoming chairman of both companies.

It was soon clear that the Austin Hall Group was in fairly desperate shape, and it was not surprising that it had so quickly accepted my offer of help. In the early days of the relationship the chairman of Austin Hall, James Austin, scion of one of the founding families, came to see me in my office in City Wall House. He came purposefully into the room, and, as he carefully took off his gloves, he spoke. 'I said to my butler this morning,' he declared, 'City today; B, B and B – brolly, briefcase, and best overcoat.' It really was a very different world. During 1970 and 1971 I was spending one to two days a week on Austin Hall business, playing the role of a part-time but very involved chairman. The loss-making joinery businesses were closed down; the garden shed and greenhouse business and the nascent system-building division were both strengthened by acquisition; and a motor car hire purchase subsidiary (which had been developed for no very good reason) was run down to generate cash which would finance further expansion in the other parts of the group. The share price increased fourfold in the two-year period; this certainly beat making grinding wheels at Carborundum's Trafford Park factory in Manchester; and the City and the financial press had taken notice.

The development of Marshall Morgan and Scott was on a more modest scale. Its original business was tiny and specialist in the extreme; it published religious books of a fundamentalist Protestant persuasion; hardly the business for an Irish Catholic accountant working for a Jewish banker. It struggled to make a profit of £20,000 a year, but it was my unlikely introduction to the book trade. We looked for opportunities to make other publishing acquisitions and purchased World Distributors and Ward Lock. World Distributors published mass market children's books (particularly children's annuals) whilst Ward Lock was a more conventional and respected member of the book trade establishment, publishing books on gardening, cookery (including Mrs Beeton), travel (the Red Guides), hobbies, and children's and educational books. We had the makings of a small, but interesting specialist publishing group – and again it caught the imagination of the stock market with a threefold increase in its share price.

At the end of 1971, I had been on the main board of FNFC for a year and I was sharing one enormous office with Pat and with John Black, who was the director responsible for FNFC's extensive property interests. I had delegated the financial control responsibilities to a newly appointed controller whom I had recruited from outside the City and I spent most of my time running the investment banking activities of FNFC (which included the investments in Austin Hall and Marshall Morgan and Scott) for which I was responsible. My relationship with Pat ran the whole gamut of his highly emotional and volatile personality. There would be times when he would insist that I joined him on a Sunday at his country house in Wargrave so that we could talk and then drive into London together on the Monday morning; or, if he was staying in town, he would often telephone me on a Sunday morning to suggest that we walked together over Hampstead Heath. He would discuss the same issues and personalities endlessly, which was wearing and frustrating. Nothing ever appeared to be settled and I found it difficult to make any firm plan; it seemed to me that he was a master at creating insecurity and that one piece of the jigsaw was always missing and that he was the only person who knew where it was. On other occasions, he would be morose and unfriendly, and I would consider myself lucky that my responsibilities often took me out of the office and that the nature of my work provided in itself sufficient motivation and satisfaction.

The large office which we shared together was part of his dream of establishment, banking, respectability; it represented the traditional partners' parlour of the blue-chip merchant banker. Given the personalities involved, it was certainly not an efficient or productive workplace; and John Black was only slightly less volatile and emotional than Pat Matthews. When receiving a telephone call I would often feel that two other pairs of ears were cocked to catch the hint of any new problem; or I would find it impossible to hear my caller through the shouting match then taking place between Pat and John. Grievances grew, real or imagined, and one day things were said on both sides which could not easily be taken back; we agreed that I would leave. I would arrange to realise a large part of the profit for FNFC on its investments in Austin Hall and Marshall Morgan and Scott – and then I would set up my own business.

The two and a half years I spent at FNFC were invaluable. Before that time I had never actually physically been into the City, and knew nothing of its ways or of its people. Now I had met and formed good working relationships with stockbrokers, fund managers, merchant bankers, corporate lawyers and some of the top investigating accountants; more importantly I had won their trust and confidence; their support and advice would be critical if I was to be successful in building an entirely new company from scratch. One of the people with whom I worked closely at FNFC was William Sanders, and he now left with me to join me at Pentos. William's background could not have been more different from my own; he was an Old Etonian, Guards officer, who had qualified as an accountant before choosing, somewhat surprisingly, to start his City career at FNFC. Now, equally surprisingly, he had decided to throw in his lot with me. His connections, knowledge of the City, and his level-headed advice were of enormous help in the early formative years of Pentos's existence; he became a director of Pentos and remained on the board until 1980.

In January 1972, Pentos was still little more than a name on the top of the notepaper. The overhead costs, including my own salary, were covered by the income from the service agreements I had entered into with Austin Hall and Marshall Morgan and Scott. However, the capital position was fairly precarious. The opening balance sheet read: assets, represented by shares in Austin Hall and Marshall Morgan and Scott, £250,000; bank debt £200,000; net worth (effectively the placing fee) £50,000. I was already a little nervous about the guarantee which I had given to the bank to secure the loan and was not anxious to take on more debt. Pentos (which at that time meant myself, William Sanders and my secretary) would have a role to play in advising Austin Hall and Marshall Morgan and Scott on their own expansion plans, but it would not be possible for Pentos itself to progress on a broader front without access to longer-term funding. A number of ideas were examined, but one particular proposal was put forward with some persistence, despite my own initial strong reservations.

The Cape Town and District Gas Light and Coke Company Limited was established in 1890 to build and operate a gas utility supplying the city of Cape Town with coal gas through 150 miles of pipelines. In 1972 the gas works was still operating, but, despite the fact that its business was in South Africa, the company was quoted in London and its shares were traded on the London Stock Exchange. It was a relic of Empire. It was a small company with 400,000 shares of £1 each, whose price in the stock market was around their par value to give a total market capitalisation of £400,000. Despite its relative unimportance it had a heavyweight board of City luminaries including Harry Sporborg of Hambros who had a reputation as the City take-over specialist at that time; and its chairman was Colonel Barstow, who was chairman of a number of other companies of faded glory as well as being a director of the Prudential Assurance Company. Two investors had built up a sizeable shareholding in the company but had run out of money with which to buy more shares and of ideas as to what to do next. They approached me with the proposal that we joined forces and then purchased further shares in the market; there were shares available from other disillusioned shareholders whose aggressive plans had also run out of steam; 'stale bulls' is, I believe, the stock exchange jargon for their predicament. We would then go to the board, from a position of considerable strength, to ask its support for an offer to be made to all its shareholders (a take-over bid) and at the same time suggest that the company acquired from me my interest in Pentos for further shares (effectively, a reverse take-over bid). The proposal had a number of attractive features for Pentos: it would obtain a stock market quotation which would enable it to pursue its expansion plans more quickly; assuming (and this was a very big assumption) that we could realise the assets at book value and repatriate the funds from South Africa to the UK, we would have substantial cash at our disposal (whereas the company's stock market value was only £400,000 and the offer we were contemplating was £500,000, the book value of the assets of the company was £1 million – we would be buying the assets at a 50 per cent discount); £160,000 of the company's assets was already in cash (equivalent to 40p per share) and we would have immediate access to this – there were no borrowings; and, last but by no means least, I would be able to secure my release from the bank guarantee which I had given in respect of Pentos's borrowings. My reservations were entirely to do with South Africa; the last thing I wanted was to have a continuing investment in a country pursuing racist policies. However, I allowed myself to be persuaded that we would be able to sell the South African interests reasonably quickly; I agreed to approach the board of the Cape Town and District Gas Light and Coke Company Limited, and to seek a meeting with its chairman.

I recall no more than two meetings with Colonel Barstow. The timing of our approach was perfect as he was about to announce reduced profits of £6,500 (this was not an exciting company), which would leave the dividend of £22,500 uncovered, and he was fearful of the reaction from his shareholders. At our first meeting he raised the question of his forthcoming trip to Cape

Town. He explained that he and his wife made an annual pilgrimage to South Africa on company business and asked for my agreement to this year's trip; he was reluctant to contemplate the prospect of explaining to his wife that it might have to be cancelled. I confirmed that I could see no reason why he should not continue as planned, and, with that out of the way, we quickly reached agreement on all of my proposals including the acquisition of Pentos by the issue of further shares in his company. The second meeting was after the completion of the formalities. He said to me that he assumed that I would myself be arranging to visit Cape Town to see at first hand the gas undertaking for which I would then be responsible. He added, in all innocence, that he was sure that I would be impressed with the new gasometer which was currently being installed; it then became clear that more than half of the cash balances which we had been eagerly anticipating was being invested in improving the gas storage facilities; this was before the days of due diligence and full disclosure, and there had been no reference to the proposed investment in the previous year's report and accounts.

The transaction brought about a dramatic transformation in the fortunes of Pentos. The agreement was announced in May 1972, and approved by shareholders on June 9, 1972. The name of the listed company was changed from the Cape Town and District Gas Light and Coke Company Limited to Pentos Limited and I was appointed chairman; in just four months, Pentos had obtained its stock market quotation – almost a candidate for the *Guinness Book of Records*. A rough balance sheet immediately after the changes would have shown total assets of about £1.2 million less net borrowings of £100,000 to give shareholders funds of £1.1 million; much depended on how successful we were in quickly realising the South African assets and converting them into sterling; but we now had shares in a quoted company which could be used as take-over currency and a balance sheet virtually free of debt; we were on our way.

Personally, I was now free of the bank guarantee and I had a large shareholding in a public company of which I was chairman and chief executive. The bank had been happy to release me from the guarantee as the borrowings had now been assumed by a public company which, relative to the debt, had a substantial asset base. I resolved never again to offer my personal guarantee for any borrowings and I have stuck to that; I had been fortunate in securing my release so quickly, but bank guarantees, rashly entered into without sufficient thought as to the possible consequences should the guarantee need to be relied upon, are responsible for most personal bankruptcies. I had obtained the original £200,000 loan from Barclays Bank because of the relationships which I had established when lunching at the bank on Austin Hall business. To lend £200,000 against the security of shares with a market value of £250,000 in two quoted companies, and a personal guarantee of doubtful value, was hardly a blue-chip banking proposition; however, the regional director of the bank had been intrigued by the ideas I had put to him for the development of my own business, and he had been impressed by my cheek in insisting on a decision the same day; he had agreed to make the loan which, in retrospect, looked just a little imprudent. I needed his help again to enable me to make the offer to the shareholders of the Cape Town and District Gas Light and Coke Company Limited. Before the bid could be made, I had to show that, should all of the shareholders accept the cash offer for their shares (other than the shares already held by the bidding consortium), I had the cash resources available to meet it in full. I spoke to my man at Barclays and explained that I would need a bank facility of £250,000 for this purpose; I also had the difficult task of explaining to him that the facility would almost certainly not be used as I expected that the share price would rise significantly above the offer price and shareholders would not accept; the stock market would recognise that, as a result of what was in effect a reverse take-over, the company had become a 'special situation' from which fireworks would be expected. He heard me with what appeared to me to be total incomprehension and also absorbed the fact that I again required a decision within twenty-four hours. He came back later the same day to say that it was all agreed, and I dictated to him the form of letter which would be required by the Stock Exchange. Barclays was heroic; but things have since changed.

The share price performed as I had forecast. Our offer price for each £1 share was 125p, which compared to the market price immediately before the offer of 100p; the stock market price immediately rose to 350p and, not surprisingly, there were no takers for the offer. This suited us perfectly as we already had sufficient shares for our purpose due to the shares already owned prior to the offer being made, and the shares being issued to me to acquire my interest in Pentos; it was also important for there to be a wide range of other shareholders for a continuation of the Stock Exchange quotation – and the quotation was critical to our future plans.

102,758 shares of £1 each were issued as the consideration for Pentos. As they were issued at the assumed price of 125p per share, the same as the offer price, the total value of the consideration was £128,448, which equated to the net worth at the date of acquisition. This net worth had increased from the initial £50,000 in January as a result of increased share prices in Austin Hall and Marshall Morgan and Scott (where we had not been inactive); the high financial gearing had meant that a 30 per cent increase in the share prices had brought about a 150 per cent increase in net worth – high gearing is not always a bad thing. When the various transactions had been completed (which included a reallocation of the shares held prior to the offer being made), I received as my own personal entitlement 116,334 shares of £1 each in the public company, which was now called Pentos. As part of the reorganisation, each £1 share was split into 10 shares of 10p each and so my personal holding became 1,163,340 shares. The total number of shares in issue was now four million and, as, in the middle of 1972, the share price had settled at 40p, the total market capitalisation of Pentos was £1.6 million, and my 29 per cent stake was valued at £465,000. The £50,000 net worth of six months ago was now being valued by the stock market at almost half a million pounds (equivalent to three million pounds in today's values); it all seemed too easy. The fact was, of course, that I could not without difficulty have sold shares at that time to realise the 'paper' profit even if I had wanted to; but that was the last thing on my mind. I was determined to build a serious business for the longer term; this was going to be no 'flash in the pan' – we were not embarking on a simple get-rich-quick scheme. (A 1979 one-for-one scrip issue meant that my 1972 holding of 1,163,340 shares was converted into 2,326,680 shares; more than twenty years later, I still owned 2.3 million shares in Pentos.) On the stock market, as in so many areas of activity, it is better to travel than to arrive, and high expectations were now built into the buoyant Pentos share price; I was to find, not for the last time, that those expectations are not always easy to satisfy.

There have been three distinct phases in the development of Pentos and each of them has included a period of major adverse change in the economic fortunes of the country. The first phase was from its inception in 1972 to 1975. During this period, Pentos acted primarily as an investment company, holding strategic shareholdings in other quoted companies; it would seek to exercise significant influence over the policies of the companies in which it was invested and to offer financial advice; this was the pattern which had already been established with Austin Hall and Marshall Morgan and Scott; the action was in the 'satellites' rather than in Pentos. The second phase was from 1975 to 1980, when Pentos became a more conventionally structured industrial holding company. The stock market hiatus of 1974–75 had created an opportunity for Pentos to pursue a strategy of acquiring all of the shares in its various affiliates; this was generally effected by take-over bids; the action was now channelled through a number of wholly owned subsidiaries operating in diverse fields; Pentos had become a mini-conglomerate. The last phase was from 1981 to the present time. During this period, Pentos pursued a policy of divesting itself of all of its non-retailing activities so as to devote the whole of its resources to specialist retailing. To some extent, this was making a virtue of necessity, as Pentos suffered severely from the recession of 1980 to 1982 and had little option but to reduce the scale of its activities. Nonetheless, it was a conscious strategic decision to change direction in this way and, as a result, Pentos emerged a much stronger and more focused company. With the important exception of the office furniture business which is yet to be realised, this final stage of development was completed just as we entered the recession of 1990 to 1993. Pentos was now a retailer.

Although the corporate structure changed as Pentos evolved from a diversified investment company into a specialist retailer, the investment and business philosophy has been consistent throughout. The emphasis at all times has been on the market-place. Reading through annual reports, the same words and phrases recur: 'quality', 'a recognisable product', 'the potential for market leadership', 'a clear brand identity'. In the Pentos 1992 annual report the two major corporate objectives are stated as 'to earn a return on investment which is significantly better than average and to seek leadership and a clear identity in its chosen markets'. Those are the same corporate objectives which were first set twenty years ago. In most years Pentos has been successful in earning a relatively high return on investment, and I have no doubt that the substantial new investment made in recent years will, assuming no major change in trading policies, generate a more than acceptable return in the future. As far as the market-place is concerned, Pentos has developed a number of well-known, successful brands, and each has become established as a market leader: Halls Greenhouses; Dillons Bookstores; Athena Galleries; Ryman the Stationer; and, in the office furniture market, Caplan and Asher.

In the early years, the problem was identifying markets and opportunities which met our criteria. Given limited resources, it was likely that the markets would not be enormous; would not involve high technology; would be fragmented and relatively inefficient so as to facilitate easy entry and provide the opportunity to move quickly to a position of some influence and eventual leadership; and, of course, there had to be the potential for growth in the market as a whole as we were not looking to enter stagnant or declining markets.

The first moves in 1973, however, were to take two steps which added to our financial resources and which, therefore, made it easier for us to develop our ambitious plans for the real world of products and markets. In March 1973 we were able to announce the sale of the gas undertaking in Cape Town for more than £600,000, and, after tortuous exchange control negotiations, the proceeds were transferred to London. Tim Bettany, one of the original consortium members and a director of Pentos, had spent six months in Cape Town, improving profitability and looking for a buyer. Despite Tim's efforts, the business was still only marginally profitable and the sale prospectus which he showed to likely buyers assumed that the purchaser would invest in an oil conversion unit which would replace coal with oil as the basic raw material. As it was currently operated, coal was hauled across South Africa from the Transvaal and was then processed to produce town gas, which was distributed through the pipeline, and its by-product coke, which was used for heating. The plan was for oil to be used instead of coal, which would be cleaner, cheaper, and result in a more profitable business. This was the concept which had enabled Tim to drum up interest in the company and to bring about its eventual sale. Within months of the transaction being completed, the market price of oil went through the roof and the economics of the oil conversion unit were in ruins. We had been very fortunate. Overall, together with the original cash balances, and other small property interests, we had recovered the whole of the book value of the Cape Town and District Gas Light and Coke Company Limited. All of its assets were now represented by cash – and the cash was in London. It was 'mission accomplished' with a vengeance.

The second money-raising exercise was of longer-term significance and was to establish a business partnership which lasted for eighteen years and a friendship which still exists today. Philip Greer was an American venture capitalist whom I had met whilst at FNFC. He is one of the founding partners of an investment firm based in New York and, from his San Francisco office, he also advised the Bank of America on its venture capital investments. Towards the end of 1971, he had sought to persuade me to set up and manage for his firm a London office, but our discussions had been overtaken by my decision to set up in business on my own account. We continued to talk throughout 1972 of ways in which we could work together, and, in February 1973, we announced an agreement under which the funds under Philip's management and the Bank of America venture capital subsidiary would together invest £740,000 in our small company. The deal was complicated as my new American friends did not wish to be contaminated by the South African business, the sale of which had not yet been completed, but effectively the two investors each had a 10 per cent shareholding in the non-South African interests. It was quite a coup. Philip joined our board, and we had as a major shareholder the largest bank in the world (which it then was); I believe that the Pentos investment was the only direct investment held by the Bank of America in a UK company.

The oil price explosion of late 1973 did not only affect the economics of the proposed gas works conversion; it precipitated a major meltdown in world financial markets. The *Financial Times* ordinary share index, which in 1972 had been more than 500, touched a low of 146 in January 1975 (in May 1994 it is around 2,500); the Bank of England minimum lending rate had increased to 13 per cent from 5 per cent; and UK commercial property prices declined in many cases by between one-third and one-half. The buoyant conditions in the UK stock market in the early Seventies had been fuelled primarily by easy access to a ready supply of relatively cheap money. Now the cost of borrowing had more than doubled, cash was no longer readily available, the financial assets on which banks had been so quick to lend – shares and property – had seen a dramatic decline in value, and, crucially, they could not be realised because there were no buyers. Each day there was news of a new financial institution rumoured to be in trouble, usually a secondary bank, and then of its failure; the Bank of England put out its now famous 'lifeboat'; the National Westminster Bank, incredibly, issued a press release to say that it was financially sound, as it apparently felt the need to reassure nervous depositors. Many of the new companies which had been launched on the stock market in the late Sixties and early Seventies, and with whom Pentos was often, I thought wrongly, compared, were to go to the wall. We were fortunate at Pentos in that we had secured a sound financial base. We had negligible borrowings, we had established a number of confidence-boosting premier league connections, and we were investing in real businesses rather than financial assets. Unlike its experience in later recessions, the heartland of UK manufacturing industry was relatively unaffected by the 'financial recession' of 1974–75 and industrialists could not understand the panic in the City – or their low share prices. The share prices of Austin Hall and Marshall Morgan and Scott, which were still Pentos's largest investments, had fallen in line with the market as a whole, even though the underlying businesses were still performing well. Pentos took full advantage of the unique opportunity created by its own relative financial strength and the aberrant stock market; offers were made to acquire all the outstanding shares in Austin Hall in 1974 and Marshall Morgan and Scott in 1975, and, despite the fact that each company was in itself substantially larger than Pentos, the bids were successful. In just two years, from the end of 1973 to the end of 1975, funds employed had increased from £1.4 million to £11.3 million; sales from £1.8 million to £29.5 million; and trading profit from £350,000 to £3 million. Pentos was now a sizeable company.

Whilst Pentos was shooting the rapids of the turbulent stock market, the 'real' businesses, which after all were its raison d'être, were not being neglected. One of the activities of Austin Hall was the manufacture of timber greenhouses and its subsequent development was an early example of a successful marketing initiative. Halls was a well-known name in a fragmented market, but little had been done to develop and exploit brand awareness. Sales were achieved primarily by mail order, through advertising in the national press and in gardening magazines, and through the use of catalogues. Sales techniques had not changed in more than twenty years and the market was unexciting, with weak demand now being exacerbated by consumer resistance to substantial increases in the price of cedar, from which the greenhouses were made. In 1974, we decided for the first time to manufacture an aluminium greenhouse to sell alongside the traditional cedar product. The advantages of the aluminium greenhouse were that it was cheaper and that it could be packaged and sold in the high street like any other consumer product. It was introduced to the Co-op, Debenhams, Tesco and many other national multiple chains. Whereas, before, the market had been confined to the garden enthusiast who had the money and determination to purchase the expensive, difficult-to-buy (it typically would take four weeks to deliver), high-quality cedar product, a cheap and cheerful aluminium alternative was now available in the high street, and, backed by national advertising, it opened up a whole new mass market. Within a year, aluminium greenhouse sales had overtaken cedar, and in two years they were 75 per cent of total greenhouse sales; more importantly the total number of greenhouse sales had doubled and Halls had secured the dominant position in the enlarged greenhouse market with more than 40 per cent market share. In 1977, Halls won the Institute of Marketing Award for outstanding achievements in British marketing.

The other business which had its origins within Austin Hall, and which became the largest UK company of its kind, was the system-building division. It manufactured factory-produced, timber-framed system buildings of all sizes ranging from small mobile units to complete schools. It supplied a wide range of markets but education and oil exploration, in the North Sea and the Middle East, were important. It was a highly cyclical business subject to the notorious vicissitudes of the construction industry; in a good year we could make a million pounds and in a bad year nothing. I never felt entirely comfortable with the industry, but, nonetheless, the business was to achieve a turnover of £10 million. In this, to some extent deal-driven, decade of diversity, we also managed to develop an important engineering division. It met our corporate requirements of having established brand names and an important niche in specialist markets, and, as with all the businesses we were to develop within Pentos, it started with an acquisition; it was to become one of the most important British manufacturers of liquid and gas control equipment and compression fittings. The book trade interests had also been achieving rapid expansion, although we were never to achieve a satisfactory level of profitability in the publishing activities of Ward Lock and World Distributors. The initial entry into bookselling had now been made with the acquisition of Hudsons bookshop in Birmingham in 1972, several new bookshops had been opened, and the crucially important purchase of Dillon's University Bookshops had been completed in 1977. At the end of 1978, in Pentos as a whole, funds employed were £17.8 million; sales were £54.8 million; and trading profit was £5 million. The Pentos share price at the end of 1978 was 113p, which compared to the original 10p in 1972 (this was before the capitalisation issue of 1979).

The Labour Government of 1974–79, during the period of Denis Healey's 'squeeze until the pips squeak' chancellorship, had introduced statutory control over the level of dividends which could be paid by companies to their shareholders. In 1979, Pentos devised a novel scheme which enabled the restriction to be avoided. Pentos made a capitalisation (or scrip) issue to its shareholders, but this was very much a capitalisation issue with a difference. A conventional scrip issue of (say) one new share for each share held will simply mean that shareholders finish up with double the number of shares they originally held; the share price, however, will have halved, as twice as many shares are in issue without any other change in the fundamentals, and the overall value of the shareholder's interest is unchanged.

Companies usually make scrip issues to improve the marketability of their shares as the lower share price looks cheaper; shareholders usually welcome the issue as the 'feel good' factor often leaks through to the share price and does therefore bring about some marginal real improvement. The Pentos proposal gave shareholders the option of electing either for additional ordinary shares or for a new class of deferred ordinary shares. The deferred shares were not entitled to dividends for ten years, at which time they would convert into two ordinary shares, and the dividends forgone by those opting for deferred shares would be available to those opting for ordinary shares. It enabled us, despite the statutory controls, to increase dividends to the ordinary shareholders by 35 per cent. Those shareholders who placed a high value on current income could elect for additional ordinary shares whilst those who preferred to sacrifice income in return for enhanced prospects of capital growth could elect for deferred shares. Everybody seemed happy, the share price responded favourably, and the proposal was lauded generally for its innovation. The *Daily Mail*, in its heyday with its City comment written by Patrick Sergeant and Neil Collins, devoted almost the whole of its City page to what it saw as a virtuoso performance.

The share price in 1979 touched 103p and, as each shareholder now had twice as many shares as a result of the capitalisation issue, this was equivalent to 206p on the old basis. In my chairman's statement, I was able to say that £10,000 invested in Pentos in 1972 was now, with the dividend income re-invested, worth £250,000; in the inevitable tables which were published to celebrate the end of the decade of the Seventies, Pentos was ranked the third best performing company in the stock market as a whole, and third in earnings per share growth;

we had strengthened our board by the appointment of Victor Blank, a City solicitor, and Jim Clark, one of our key executives, as directors; I concluded my statement by saying, 'Our record in the 1970s, on most measures of performance, placed Pentos amongst the leading UK companies of the decade. We believe that our prospects for the 1980s, from a base which is now established and stable, are no less exciting.' Hubris is a word I was about to get to know well.

The recession which was to destroy irrevocably much of Britain's industrial capacity was already looming on the horizon. The Conservative Party had been elected in May 1979 under the leadership of Margaret Thatcher and she appointed, as her first Chancellor, Geoffrey Howe. Interest rates had been increased to 17 per cent (they had been 6½ per cent only a year earlier), and in his first budget, in June 1979, the rate of value added tax was increased from 8 per cent to 15 per cent. Some saw it as a necessary purgative, but to others it looked like irresponsible, doctrinaire sado-masochism. The impending recession, therefore, would have been difficult enough for Pentos to negotiate, but it was exacerbated by a self-inflicted wound.

In May 1979, I received a telephone call from Panton Corbett, a managing director of Singer and Friedlander, one of the smaller merchant banks. He had a proposal he wished to put to me and it was agreed that we would meet in my office. His proposal was that Pentos should acquire Caplan Profile Group Limited, a manufacturer of office furniture and domestic upholstered furniture, for whom he acted. Pentos's acquisitions had usually been either poorly managed businesses, which in other respects matched our business criteria, and which had significant potential for improvement, or small companies which gave us a toe-hold in markets in which we could then expand. Caplan was a larger, more mature business, which had already established a significant niche in its chosen markets, and which was apparently well managed; it had reported profits of £1.1 million on sales of £6.2 million in its last completed year, and higher profits were expected in the current year. Clearly, if we were to acquire Caplan, it would be outside the normal pattern. There were, however, certain attractions: industry sources suggested that the prospects for growth over the next decade in the office furniture market in the UK and Europe were particularly good, and Caplan had a key position in what was still a fragmented market; the existence of a strong, established management team reduced risk; and finally, and this suggested an element of opportunism on our part, it appeared that the company could be acquired on advantageous terms. I met the chairman of Caplan, Ian Caplan, and subsequently his colleagues, and the basis for a deal was soon agreed. There were two important matters of principle which I stipulated: that our auditors would have access to and would review Caplan's books and accounts (which at that time was highly unusual in bids for public companies), the results of which they would then report to Pentos; and that Caplan would make a formal profit forecast of its results for the year to August 31, 1979 to Stock Exchange standards, which would therefore require the support of its auditors and of its merchant bank. The review by our auditors raised a number of minor issues which resulted in a re-negotiation of the bid terms in favour of Pentos; there were, however, no matters of substance, although it was clear that Caplan's accounting records left a lot to be desired, something I found a little unsettling. After a full discussion by the Pentos main board, the deal was confirmed, and, on July 13, 1979, it was announced that Pentos was to acquire Caplan in a share exchange offer which valued Caplan at £7 million; Caplan had forecast profits of £1.4 million for the year ending August 31, 1979.

On August 30, 1979, Ian Caplan asked to see me on a matter of great urgency. He came into my office in the middle of the afternoon in a distressed condition. We sat together around a coffee table and he tried several times to talk but had difficulty getting the words out; tears were streaming down his face. I gave him time to recover and he gradually composed himself. He then told me his story. The Caplan finance director had been to see him that morning, he said, and had informed Ian that the stock levels in the Caplan accounts had been inflated over a number of years; the result was that reported profits had been seriously overstated; a physical stock-take was due to take place the following day, under Pentos supervision, when all would have been revealed. Ian said that he had no previous knowledge of the discrepancies and that no individual had benefited financially. The finance director was later to contradict this version of events and to produce a statement which had been lodged with his solicitor in a sealed envelope some time ago. Whatever the truth of the matter was, and it was never clearly established, we had, at the very least, a major embarrassment on our hands. Independent accountants were brought in to carry out a full-scale investigation. The summary of their findings was that the net assets of Caplan showed a shortfall of £950,000 as a result of the stock overstatement, and, against the profit forecast of £1.4 million made in July 1979 in respect of a year ending only one month later, the actual profit was £769,000. The assumptions on which Pentos had agreed to acquire Caplan – that it was a well-managed, highly profitable business – had been turned on their head; we had seriously overpaid for a company that was fundamentally flawed; and the recession was to prove an unhelpful backdrop against which to put things right. Much of the next three years was to be spent in pursuing claims against those who it was thought bore some responsibility for Pentos's loss, and in bringing new management into and re-shaping the Caplan business.

The legal actions took up a large part of my own time and an even larger part of my emotional and mental resources; it was an enormous distraction in what was to be a most critical period for Pentos, with many (which never included me) doubting its ability to survive; but we could not afford to fail in pressing our claims as the figures involved were large, and failure would also have meant responsibility not only for our own legal costs but for those of our adversaries.

The legal issues involved matters such as whether advisers to Caplan owed a duty of care to Pentos and the extent to which Pentos had relied upon representations made in the course of negotiations. These were matters of principle which had not been tested in a court of law before. I seemed to live with our solicitors and established a direct line with our brilliant leading counsel Richard Scott (now Lord Justice Scott of the Matrix-Churchill enquiry fame). The culmination was a week spent sitting in the Royal Courts of Justice in the Strand. Finally, however, on October 11, 1982, it was all over; the final claim had been settled, although no legal or any other liability was accepted; all the payments were made on an ex gratia basis and the total amount received by Pentos from all the actions was

£1.6 million, of which £750,000 was from Caplan's former directors.

Caplan's management had been demoralised by the disclosure of the discrepancies. Ian Caplan and the finance director had both resigned, and Ian's brother, who was the sales director, was also to resign, at his own request, shortly after. In the short term, we had to call upon existing Pentos management resources, but these were already thinly spread; we had been led to believe that Caplan was a well-managed business and would not, therefore, require significant support. This was all happening whilst its market conditions were deteriorating rapidly. We acted as quickly as we could to improve financial control and to respond to the sharp fall in demand. Jim Clark, a Pentos main board director, assumed overall responsibility for Caplan, which he retained until the recruitment of Brian Matthews in 1981. We took the decision to concentrate Caplan's business on office furniture manufacture and withdrew from the domestic upholstered furniture market; we closed the London headquarters and factory and relocated everything to existing facilities in Ripley in Derbyshire; the overall cost base was reduced very substantially. Despite all of this, significant trading losses were incurred for the next three years, which added severely to the burdens which Pentos was already bearing. However, we never lost confidence in the future of the basic office furniture business, and, even when overhead costs were under most pressure, we did not neglect to invest in marketing and product development, on which we worked closely with our more important customers. In 1983 Caplan returned to profit, and Pentos was subsequently to invest large sums of money in building new manufacturing, warehousing and office facilities at Ripley, and in developing an entirely new systems furniture company which was named Asher. Under Brian Matthews's leadership, Caplan and Asher became the second largest manufacturer of office furniture in Britain, and a highly successful business.

There were two other significant events in the Pentos story which took place before the full force of the recession, which started in the middle of 1980, became clear. On June 6, 1980, it was announced that Pentos had reached agreement with interests controlled by Lord Rayne and his family for the subscription by them of £4 million for new equity and loan capital in Pentos. Max Rayne had made a lot of money out of property in the previous thirty years, primarily by following the simple policy of securing long-term debt at fixed rates of interest when interest rates were low. He stood out as a pillar of fiscal prudence when the nouveaux property developers of the time were buying property financed by short-term borrowings at ruinous interest rates from secondary and tertiary so-called banks, in the expectation of a never-ending price spiral. He had stood the test of time, whilst most of the others had gone to the wall. Philip Greer's investment firm in New York managed funds for Max Rayne and indirectly he had become a shareholder in Pentos through Philip's venture capital holding. Philip had introduced me to Max earlier in the year, and Max had said that should there be an opportunity to acquire a larger shareholding in Pentos would I please let him know. Bearing this in mind, I arranged to have lunch with him in the Connaught Grill in May. I explained to him that I would like to reduce Pentos's borrowings. The financial markets were unsettled, banks were cautious, clearing bank base rates had now hit the record level of 17 per cent, and business generally was becoming more difficult. We quickly sketched out a deal on the back of an envelope. Max become an equity partner in Pentos with more than 10 per cent of the enlarged capital whilst Pentos secured valuable long-term funds on attractive terms; the shares were issued at a premium to the market price whereas, if the more conventional route (assuming it were available) of a rights issue or placing with institutions had been followed, it would have been necessary to issue shares at a discount. It was to prove a highly fortuitous fund-raising exercise for Pentos and, ultimately, a very rewarding investment for Max Rayne.

The other significant event of 1980 was the acquisition in September of English and Overseas Investments Limited, a quoted UK company with two subsidiaries, Athena and Metalair. Metalair was an important manufacturer of dry bulk tankers for lorries which was of no long-term interest to Pentos and which was eventually sold in April 1983 for £1.4 million. The reason for making an offer for English and Overseas was to acquire Athena and as the value of our bid was £2.5 million, and we subsequently recouped £1.4 million from the sale of Metalair, the net cost of Athena to Pentos was little more than £1 million. Athena had been launched in 1964 as a poster and print company and had recently moved into greetings cards. There have been some who have described Athena as a 'Sixties concept'; their successors called it a 'Seventies concept'; and then there were those who thought it 'not relevant to the Eighties'. It could well be that students who were aware of the Athena product when at university (in whichever decade) have it locked in their minds, into that particular time capsule. The fact is that Athena's sales in the Sixties were minute and it had little exposure outside London. As late as 1976, sales were still less than £2 million, and, at the time of the take-over in

1980, they were £5 million. Athena was to achieve its growth, high-profile brand awareness, and success in the Eighties, when it made an important contribution to Pentos's fortunes with total sales approaching £50 million. However, any plans for expansion which existed at the time of the take-over in 1980 had to be put on ice as the financial pressures built up, and it was not until 1983 that we could again give some thought to their implementation.

At the Pentos annual general meeting in June 1980 I stated that 'the problems currently being faced by the manufacturing sector are, in many ways, as serious as those faced by the financial and property sectors in 1974–75'. That turned out to be no exaggeration. The difference so far as Pentos was concerned was that, unlike the situation which existed in 1974, we had invested most heavily in the areas which were now hardest hit. The recession was to last three years; and, although statistically the 1990–93 recession was to be deeper and to last longer, the 1980–82 recession was of unparalleled severity in terms of its relative concentration on one sector and on one part of the country. Put bluntly, it hit people who worked in factories and who lived in the North. The lethal combination of record interest rates and an overvalued currency (sustained both by the malign influence of North Sea oil and the high rates of interest available on sterling deposits), together with the increase in value added tax, brought much of manufacturing industry to its knees; and smoke-stack Britain is in the North and the Midlands; the South was relatively unscathed. Many well-known companies with an illustrious past were to go to the wall; and factories were to close, never to re-open. To visit, in 1982, parts of the Midlands and the North-West and North-East of

England was literally to travel through the industrial wastelands; it was a thoroughly dispiriting experience. Most of Pentos's businesses were engaged in manufacturing activities of one sort or another and, as luck would have it, of the non-manufacturing interests, most of our bookshops were in the Midlands and the North. In addition, Pentos had the legacy of high borrowings from the rapid but successful expansion in the 1970s, and, of course, we had to cope with the distraction of the Caplan litigation. Overall, Pentos was ill-equipped to deal with the sickening downwards lurch which was felt across all its businesses; consumers sat on their hands, retailers and wholesalers ran down their stocks, the high exchange rate meant that overseas customers found British goods to be uncompetitive, and manufacturers ceased to invest in new equipment. In 1980, Pentos reported losses for the first time in its short life. Although a trading profit of a little more than £1 million was earned, this was swamped by interest charges of more than £3 million as a result of the combination of high borrowings and high interest rates; a loss of more than £2 million was incurred and it was to be three years before Pentos returned to profit; those three years were to be the worst of my business life.

Some two weeks before we were due to announce our results to the Stock Exchange, we informed our bankers of the likely outcome, as a matter of courtesy; the last thing we wanted was for them to read the bad news for the first time in the newspapers. Within hours, the Pentos finance director received a telephone call from a Mr Carslake at Barclays Bank; the message was direct and delivered in an apparently brutal manner: he was to get hold of his chairman straightaway and we were both to attend upon him at his office in the City. Stan

Carslake has the appearance of a rather unsuccessful boxer. He has a battered-looking, large-featured, lived-in face, and a head which looks a little too big for its five-foot-two body; in between chain-smoking cigarettes, he continually moistens his lips. He was proud of having been born within the sound of Bow Bells, and therefore an authentic cockney. All in all he was a most unlikely top banker. Like many men (but not women) of small stature he over-compensates with raw aggression, and, on occasion, he would use his power base at Barclays Bank to devastating effect. Initially, I thought him the most unpleasant man I had ever met but I slowly warmed to him, and beneath his bluster, as is so often the case, he was nowhere near as tough as he thought; he was to become a valuable ally.

It seemed to me at that first meeting with Stan Carslake that his objective was one of simple intimidation. The bank will call the shots now, he said, and it would want an independent investigation by accountants, a legal charge over all the assets of the company, and control over many aspects of its business – not least capital expenditure, which, he assumed, would in any event now be a thing of the past; the business must be run for cash was his message. He clearly knew little about Pentos and he seemed unimpressed by what he did know; he was far from convinced that it had a future. The shock tactics, I was to discover, were part of his stock in trade. We had been accompanied to the meeting by the regional director of Barclays who handled the Pentos account. It was not the original regional director who had been so 'heroic' at the time that Pentos was launched, as he had sadly retired; his successor was of a quite different mettle, and, although Stan Carslake's aim was to frighten me and my finance director, what he most certainly did do was to put the fear of God into the regional director. He hardly uttered a word, and his ever-open, free-lending, smiling-faced door was now closed to us; we would in the future deal exclusively with Stan Carslake.

Stan's first move was to speak to all the other lenders to Pentos and then to get them together for a meeting which was to be addressed by me. Prior to the meeting, the Pentos finance director provided Barclays, who were to act as the lead bank, with detailed budgets and with schedules of existing bank facilities, likely level of future borrowings, and, most importantly, the steps which we were taking to reduce borrowings, including the disposal of certain 'peripheral' assets and businesses. The meeting was attended by the 12 to 14 banks with whom Pentos had borrowings. It was an unfriendly gathering and most of the faces were new to me; those who had been happily lending the money had now gone and we were dealing with those who wanted it back. I immediately became aware of the problems of multi-banking relationships; there were far too many banks (it was a mistake which we were not to repeat) and it was not going to be easy to reach unanimity. Each bank was obsessively concerned to protect its own interests and the interests of Pentos did not come into the reckoning (Barclays and the Midland were eventually to prove to be exceptions to this, although cynics might argue that, as they had most at stake, they had more reason to be supportive); the American banks and the British merchant banks were the least co-operative and simply wanted to take whatever money they could get and run; fear and greed have long been the twin dominant emotions in the City, and we were now seeing fear's unveiled and ugly face. I was not going to be cowed; I berated them and pointed to their inconsistency in first bombarding us with aggressive marketing to take on more debt, and then turning tail and running at the first sound of grapeshot; another example of the banks taking away your umbrella as soon as it starts to rain. I touched on the problems caused by the recession (which should have been of no surprise to them) and the steps which we were taking to improve profitability and reduce debt; I said that I was convinced of the prospects for recovery and determined to bring it about. They did not look noticeably more friendly although I did receive smiles of encouragement from the few faces which I knew. The Pentos contingent then withdrew and the banks deliberated together under the resolute chairmanship of Stan Carslake.

That first meeting was inconclusive. There was apparently widespread scepticism about our ability to generate the cash from disposals which we had projected. However, we were able to receive sufficient comfort from the banks to issue our trading results to the Stock Exchange, which had been our primary short-term objective. Over the next few months I was able to see Stan Carslake in operation at close quarters, and to appreciate his positive qualities. When bankers' heads needed banging together he would approach the task with obvious relish and with a coarseness of language which left some of the more delicate merchant bank lenders looking a little sick. He resisted all attempts by other banks to impose additional costs on Pentos by, for example, higher margins on interest rates or facility fees; he was determined that they should not add further burdens which could jeopardise our recovery. Stan Carslake, in turn, was impressed by our efforts to reduce borrowings, although we were initially less successful in improving profits. His ability at controlling the in-fighting between banks meant that we had the one commodity without which we would have failed, and that was time. The bank facilities which existed at the beginning of 1981 were sufficient to cover the projected borrowing levels and we did not, therefore, have the embarrassment of having to ask for additional facilities; requests for further borrowings, usually to finance short-term working capital requirements, are often the catalyst which leads to precipitate action from the banks; so far as we were concerned we simply had to ensure that existing banking arrangements were kept in place. The plans which we had put forward for asset disposals showed a gradual reduction in borrowing levels; we just needed the time to bring about those realisations without any undue pressure; it must not seem to the outside world as if we were engaged in a fire sale. Stan Carslake soon came to see that if the banks wanted an orderly realisation of the assets of the business then existing management would do a better job than anybody else. So far as we were concerned, the key thing was to stay in control and not allow ourselves to be swayed from our own strategic objectives; we must not be pressurised into selling any business which featured in our longer-term plans – we must not sell the 'crown jewels'. Over the next three years, we disposed of all of our engineering activities, which included the flotation on the Stock Exchange of its principal business, Jeavons Engineering, and which realised in total £3.5 million; we sold Halls to its management to bring in a total of £4 million (the development role played by Pentos was at an end and Halls was now operating in a mature market); we withdrew entirely from construction and sold all of the book publishing interests. Tony Hazard, who was then a managing director of Pentos, was in overall charge of the realisation programme and he did a fantastic job. We realised figures which astonished Stan Carslake and won his trust and admiration. Borrowings which had been £15 million at the start of 1981, and which peaked at close to £20 million shortly after, were reduced to £7 million by the end of 1983; two years later they had been reduced further to £4 million. Pentos returned to profit in 1983, although the figure was only a modest £287,000; in 1984 it rose to £1.8 million and in 1985 to £3 million. The profile of the business was now clearly visible with the emphasis on its specialist retailing activities; the property and office furniture interests would be realised at some suitable future date. On the back of the reduced borrowings, the strengthened balance sheet, and the improved profits, Pentos launched a rights issue in April 1986 to raise £10 million; we again had cash in the bank, and we were now ready to develop further our retail concepts.

The Pentos share price had fallen to a low of 6p in 1982 at a time when there were many in the City who thought that our struggles against the recession might well prove terminal; this compared to the equivalent of 5p at the time of the reversal into the Cape Town and District Gas Light and Coke Company Limited in 1972, and the high (at that time) of 103p achieved in 1979. By the end of 1985, the share price had recovered to 63p, and it was at this level that the April 1986 rights issue was struck; during the course of the year, the share price rose further to 87p. It was the first rights issue which Pentos had made. Rights issues should be launched from a position of strength, and the timing had therefore been important; Pentos now had a good story to tell, its finances were in good shape, and the market was just beginning to get a whiff of the retail 'story'; it is always easier to get something if you can show that you don't really need it.

It was inevitable that the original scatter-gun approach

to investment by Pentos would develop more into that of a rifle. Pentos started life as an investment company with a narrow financial base and the absolute necessity of spreading risk. With time, and the knowledge which only comes with ownership, some investments look better than others; external factors can also change and so challenge the validity of previous assumptions; and I was always aware of the development role to be played by Pentos with the recognition that there might come a time in the life of a particular business when that role would end and a new owner might be more appropriate. So it was no surprise that there were divestments along the way, and the banking problems of the early 1980s merely hurried the process along. Pentos now increasingly saw its future as a specialist retailer, and that is how it was perceived by the stock market.

In the early stages of this new emphasis on retailing, it was Athena rather than Dillons which made the running. Athena's product offer was developed in the early Eighties to feature strong air-brushed imagery on its posters and greetings cards; it was a particular success with the fashion-conscious young, and became very much a part of the teenage culture of the time. The retail environment in which the product was sold, however, was still rooted in the Sixties. A retail design consultant, Jon Isherwood, had been commissioned to produce a new design concept for the Athena galleries which would complement the highly visual contemporary product range and at the same time create a more exciting presence on the high street. The first, newly designed gallery opened in King Street in Manchester towards the end of 1983. It was an immediate success, and, with some modifications, it formed the basis for the start of a roll out of a national chain of Athena galleries. In the UK, the original chain of 24 galleries was converted to the new design between 1984 and 1986, and sales showed an immediate increase of 30 per cent solely as a result of the new look and improved fixturing. A major expansion programme was announced and by the end of 1986 there were 48 galleries and by the end of 1988 77 galleries. In the period 1983 to 1986, Athena was the star performer in the Pentos firmament; institutional shareholders who came to lunch with me would press me to change the Pentos name to Athena, and the covers of the 1984 and 1986 Pentos annual reports featured Athena almost exclusively; how fashions change, and how short are memories. It was, however, soon to be Dillons' turn to capture the imagination of the stock market. The Gower Street store was refurbished to great acclaim in 1986, the first new Dillons was opened in Oxford in 1987, and that was the start of the Dillons chain. In 1986, Pentos's profits increased by 68 per cent to £5 million, beating by 25 per cent the previous, pre-recession, record achieved in 1978; at the end of the year, there were still no bank borrowings, although the investment programme was now beginning to build up; sales were £63 million, of which 61 per cent were from retail activities. The share price, which peaked at 87p in 1986, reached an all-time high of 184p in the middle of 1987; this was due mainly to continued stock market interest in Pentos's emerging retail concepts, and only to a small extent to a stronger stock market.

2

Dillons the Bookstore

The Dillons story for me began in August 1977 with the acquisition of Dillon's University Bookshops; but the story of 'Dillons the Bookstore' starts in 1986 with the transformation of that landmark building in Bloomsbury, bounded by Malet Street, Torrington Place and Gower Street, from a university bookshop supplying the needs of London University into a bookshop of much wider appeal.

Truman Capote, when travelling to Russia with the cast of the American production of *Porgy and Bess* in 1956, described in *The Muses Are Heard* his first Russian shopping experience. He had chosen a hat.

> A fake astrakhan, it cost $45; and because of the complicated payment system that operates in all Soviet stores, from the humblest grocery to GUM's in Moscow, it required another forty minutes to complete the transaction. First, the clerk gives you a sales slip, which you carry to a cashier's booth – when the money has been paid, the cashier stamps the sales slip, and this you take back to the clerk, who by now

> is attending to five other people; eventually, though, the clerk will accept the slip, go to check it with the cashier, come back, hand over your purchase, and direct you to a wrapping department, where you join another queue. At the end of this process, I was given my hat in a green box.

Those familiar with the Charing Cross Road will immediately recognise Foyle's, the world's most famous bookshop. The main difference would be that in Russia the sales assistants might well have spoken English. Foyle's is an extreme example, but there is no doubt that the retail revolution which had swept the high streets of Britain in the Seventies and early Eighties had bypassed the book trade.

Foyle's claimed to be the largest bookshop in the world. At the beginning of the 1980s, in terms of floor space, numbers of titles and turnover, it was certainly the largest bookshop in Britain. The UK's largest bookseller, however, was W.H. Smith, although many argued that Smith's was not a real bookseller at all – one of the many snobberies of the book trade. Smith's had a large chain of stationery shops and was on every high street. It was not a specialist bookseller, but books were an important part of its product range. It carried a relatively limited range of titles, mainly bestsellers, paperbacks and activity and hobby-oriented books. Its commitment to the book trade at that time was thought to be ambiguous and uneven. It always struck me as ironic given its limited book range (particularly of literary titles) that Smith's chairman would later be the staunchest defender of the Net Book Agreement on the grounds of its central importance to the cultural heritage of the country. Nonetheless, despite its narrow range, Smith's very presence on every high street meant that it was easily the largest book retailer in the country – and many publishers would not commit to a new title without first getting a reaction from Smith's.

The John Menzies chain of stationery shops was similar to Smith's in its approach to the market, but, if anything, carried an even narrower range of titles. However, from its Scottish base, it was not even close to Smith's in terms of importance to the book trade.

The rest of the retail market (excluding book clubs) was supplied by the so-called 'independents' – the specialist bookshops; and they had by far the largest market share.

The myth lived on in certain parts of the book trade and of the media that Britain had been well served historically by a large number of independent bookshops up and down the country which had caring proprietors who knew about books, had well-stocked shelves, and would quickly offer to order any book if it was not in stock. The reality could not have been more different.

There were, of course, some good specialist bookshops, but these were mainly in the university towns: Blackwells in Oxford, Heffers in Cambridge, perhaps Thin's in Edinburgh and maybe John Smith's in Glasgow. The approach of these shops was strictly academic. They had no easy appeal to the general market. And then of course there was Hatchards in Piccadilly – but that was for the toffs.

For the rest, they were thin on the ground and extremely variable in quality. Many were in poor positions in towns where the retail trade had moved on because of redevelopment and the bookshop had been left behind. They were often far too small to carry anything like a sufficiently wide range of books; and old-fashioned and inappropriate shelving meant that they could not properly display the stock they did carry. They were under-capitalised; stock control techniques did not exist; and they were closed for lunch and on Saturday afternoons, which was when most people did their shopping. The proprietors were often eccentric individuals although many did indeed have a love of books; if you should venture into the High Hill bookshop in Hampstead and have the misfortune to deal with the irascible Ian Norrie, then you were as likely to leave with a flea in your ear as to purchase the desired book; some had thought that running a bookshop was a good thing to do in retirement almost as a hobby.

But, most importantly of all, there was little idea of the market or how to expand it. Bookshops had a narrow appeal. Most people never entered a bookshop in their lives. There was a feeling in some parts of the trade that people who buy books know what they want and know where to find what they want. And the rest didn't matter. To use a modern marketing term, bookshops were not user-friendly. Many people were intimidated at the prospect of entering a bookshop. I remember my first experience of a bookshop as a schoolboy in Manchester. I entered the shop, mentioned the title of the book I wanted and was immediately asked for the name of the publisher. I didn't know the answer – I am not sure that I knew what a publisher was – and left the shop in some confusion. Needless to say, empty-handed, without the book. Things had not changed much in the intervening thirty years.

In the hierarchy of the book trade, most publishers believe that they are definitely a cut above booksellers. A publisher has a unique product, and, if a bookseller wants to stock it, he has to deal with that publisher. If a grocer does not like the way Heinz run its business, he can transfer his custom for baked beans to another supplier, or develop his own brand. In the book trade, if a bookseller wants Stephen Hawkings' *A Brief History of Time*, he has no option but to deal with its publisher, Transworld. Publishing houses tended to be editorially led and editorially driven, production and distribution were the poor relations, and the conventional idea of marketing was a drinks party. The end result was that far too many books were published, 60,000 new titles each year; far too few copies of each title were sold; it usually took two to three weeks to get a book from a publisher's warehouse to the bookshop; and book prices were too high.

Because of an eccentric judgement of the Restrictive Practices Court in 1962, books had been exempted from the Resale Prices Act of 1964, which abolished resale price maintenance. As a result, the book trade had been excluded from the unique surge of energy and innovation which had transformed the retail landscape in Britain in the subsequent two decades. Books had continued to be protected from the full force of competition and publishers continued to set prices for their products which booksellers would vary at their peril.

So specialist bookshops were outside the mainstream of British retailing. The market was fragmented, undercapitalised, old-fashioned, snobbish, inward-looking, regulated and, not surprisingly, inefficient. And the book trade could not understand why so few people in Britain bought books. That was the state of book retailing in this country at the start of the Eighties. What an opportunity.

Dillon's University Bookshop was founded by Una Dillon in 1936. It was originally in Store Street and moved to its present situation in Malet Street in 1957 when the University of London became her partner. As the financing requirements of the expanding business became greater the University purchased Miss Dillon's shares and became the sole owner. In the 1970s the shop experienced a number of trading problems and was losing money; it also had great difficulty in meeting its obligations to its suppliers and on one well-remembered occasion a number of publishers were sufficiently concerned to send their vans to the shop to recover stock in lieu of long-delayed and increasingly doubtful payment. Una Dillon had resigned from the position of managing director although she remained on the board as a non-executive director. There had been a number of management changes but it was the trades union (a branch of the TGWU) which had increasingly become the dominant influence. The University of London was naturally concerned; it was also reviewing its policy, in those financially straitened times, towards its non-academic activities (in addition to the bookshop, it also owned a publishing house and a computer software company). A new chairman was appointed by the University to the bookshop board to improve its finances and to arrange for its sale.

Pentos had been a modest investor in book retailing since shortly after its formation in 1972 when Marshall Morgan and Scott, which became the holding company for its book trade-related activities, acquired Hudsons bookshops in Birmingham. We were, therefore, identified by Ken Stephenson, Dillon's new chairman, as a possible buyer. We were, however, by no means his first choice. Stephenson was an accountant who had recently retired after a long and successful career in publishing. He knew most people in the trade and he spoke first to those who he thought would be the most logical buyers. They were all, however, deterred by the strength of the trades union presence at Dillon's. As they have since told me, Ian Chapman would like to have bought Dillon's for Collins but was fearful that the union would then establish a stranglehold on Hatchards; and Toby Blackwell, who had long had an ambition to own a prestigious London bookshop, was even more paranoid at the prospect of trades union influence in Oxford. Pentos, therefore, although not quite the last resort, was pretty close to it.

Ken Stephenson is an affable man, and we soon established a good and constructive working relationship; a deal was quickly struck and in August 1977 we announced the purchase of Dillon's University Bookshops by Pentos for £650,000. In addition to the main shop in Bloomsbury, there were two small campus bookshops; the total turnover from these three shops was £4 million (of which £2.5 million was from Malet Street) and as Ken Stephenson had largely stemmed the losses which the business had been incurring it was poised to move into profit.

We might have appeared complacent about our ability to handle relationships with the trades union which others had found daunting. We now needed to act quickly and it was agreed that I would address a meeting of the whole of the staff (for which we had to obtain union permission). We had two objectives: we had to prevent the union representation spreading to the Hudsons bookshops until we had an acceptable basis for a relationship; and we had to re-establish the right of management to manage at Dillon's. These might sound like strong anti-trades union sentiments for a Liberal; the fact is that the abdication of responsibility by weak management had been fully exploited by the union and it was the union which ran the shop. This had to change. I found that first staff/union meeting depressing; there was open hostility and every statement I made was questioned in tones of disbelief. This sounded like war and I was the enemy.

Although the purchase of Dillon's turned into a successful acquisition and was of enormous strategic importance, we had seriously underestimated the trades union problems. It took years to overcome the smouldering suspicion and the outright obstructionism which we first encountered. Each move to improve service or performance was routinely opposed; it then became painstakingly slow to change attitudes which quickly became entrenched. It was one of the factors which made us reluctant to commit large sums of money for new investment in those early years. The issue of Saturday afternoon opening was a good example. Dillon's Malet Street shop had always closed at one o'clock on Saturdays; each week many customers still anxious to spend money on buying books were turned into the streets at Saturday lunchtime. For most retailers, Saturday is the most important day of the week, with the afternoon trading being equal to that of the morning. But the traditionalists at Dillon's argued that there were too few people in the University area on Saturday afternoon and that it would not pay to open. It took a long time before they could be persuaded to experiment. Of course, the result was predictable. Saturday sales easily became the highest of any day of the week and sales for the whole day were more than twice the level which had previously been achieved for the morning trading; apparently lunchtime closing had meant that many customers had not been prepared to make the journey to Dillon's on a Saturday and risk being asked to leave before their purchases were complete. On any measure of performance, the change was a great success; in addition to improving customer service it added significantly to the shop's profits; and it is difficult to imagine today a 'destination' store of such importance not being open at every conceivable opportunity. Trades union relationships have improved dramatically in recent years, particularly since the major investment in transforming the store in 1986; and there is on most issues a civilised and constructive dialogue; but it is still the case that it takes longer to introduce changes to routine in Malet Street/Gower Street than in almost any other shop; and it is still closed on Sundays.

The recession of 1980–82 brought a halt to any plans for the further expansion of our nascent book retailing chain; Pentos simply did not have the resources. The economic recovery, and improvement in underlying trading, and the subsequent rights issue, meant that new investment could again be resumed and the first priority was to improve the quality of our existing bookshops and, once we were satisfied that the formula was right, to add new shops to the chain. At Malet Street new space had become available as the leases of sub-tenants of Dillon's came to an end and were not renewed; the additional space was converted to bookselling. We also did a complete re-fit of our quite large shop in Nottingham (formerly named Sisson and Parker), and there were a number of more minor projects. The aim was to improve the overall appearance of the shops; to make them more welcoming; to make it easier for customers to find the books they wanted; and to introduce new shelving which by making more effective use of space would enable us to stock more books, and to display them better. Our own in-house team at Pentos worked closely with James McCartney, a firm of Nottingham architects, and there is no doubt that significant improvements were made. The quality of fittings and general retail standards in our bookshops were now a match for any other British bookseller; but that was not saying very much. In other areas of retailing, throughout the high street, there had been dramatic improvements in design, in retail concepts, and in an approach to service, which made our puny efforts look pedestrian. I felt a vague dissatisfaction and frustration with what we were doing but did not myself have the answer.

At about that time, in late 1985, Peter Gorb persuaded me to attend a lecture at the London Business School. Peter is a former retailer, having once been joint managing director of Burton's, who had moved into the academic world; he is an enthusiastic and extrovert academic. He had established a design unit at the London Business School and had organised a series of lectures on various aspects of design. One of the lectures, to be delivered by Rodney Fitch, was on retail design and, a little reluctantly, I went along. Fitch had built a reputation as perhaps Britain's most influential retail design consultant. He had worked with Terence Conran and had then left to establish his own company which had been successful and which had obtained a stock market quotation. I had not met him before the lecture and I was impressed by his total approach to design and by the slide presentation of work which he and others had done both here and in America. It convinced me that my increasing uneasiness with our own piecemeal approach was justified and that we had to find a better way forward. I called Rodney the following day and arranged to meet him in his office. I felt a little apprehensive about trying to explain to him, the retail design guru, my own ideas and vision for our bookshops when they were still not entirely or clearly formed. However, my natural enthusiasm and my certainty about the existence of a major business opportunity soon took over. We were both agreed that bookselling in Britain was still not part of mainstream retailing; and that there were rich rewards for whoever first developed a successful concept. Fitch had previously had abortive talks with Blackwells but Rodney told me that it was not now committed to any other bookseller and he was keen to work with Pentos if we wanted him. I was increasingly certain that getting the design concept right was critical to our plans; and I liked the idea of working with Rodney Fitch.

I returned to my office and immediately consulted with my colleagues; principally Frank Brazier, who was in charge of our emerging bookselling business, and Jim Clark, who was now on the main Pentos board responsible for property. Jim Clark has a natural suspicion of designers; his world consists of architects, chartered surveyors and civil engineers, and a proposal to place a building project under the overall control of a design consultant would, in his view, be a guarantee that it would fall down. He was therefore a little cautious about my enthusiastic advocacy of Fitch & Co.

We were about to embark on some further work at Dillon's in Malet Street as additional space which had previously been used as offices had become available on the second floor. The project had been authorised and the architects had already prepared plans which had been approved; this was consistent with the gradual and slightly hesitant approach to the development of the site which we had been pursuing for the past two years. It was now agreed that this further work would be put on ice. We were to stand back and look at the potential re-development of the building as a whole. If we were to proceed it would be an ambitious project; certainly the largest which we had yet undertaken. We drew up a list of those who would be invited to make presentations as part of a 'beauty parade'; it consisted mainly of architects; but Fitch was also on the list. To my surprise and embarrassment the Fitch presentation was not impressive; they had not done their homework and had not given sufficient thought to their proposals; the project was far more complicated than they had realised. Frank Brazier and Jim Clark were more tolerant and sympathetic than I had any right to expect; they recognised, as I had earlier, that, although other competitive proposals were more workmanlike and more clearly thought through, Fitch could add a dimension and flair which would not otherwise be on offer; they suggested that Fitch should come in again for further discussions. It was eventually decided that Fitch would work with McCartney, our existing architects, and it was on this basis that the project was awarded to them jointly. The real work then began. It was determined at the outset that the most important single issue was to involve fully the staff at Malet Street and to obtain their total co-operation. Fitch might be expert in retail design but it knew little about bookselling; and in many respects books *were* different. We also recognised the recent history of bad labour relations; this was an opportunity to win the support of the staff and to engage their enthusiasm. Another early decision was that the shop was not to close; the work would be carried out in three separate phases; as books and dust do not go well together (and there was going to be a lot of dust) and the noise at times would become very intrusive it was also important that we obtained the co-operation of our customers. We would keep customers fully informed of what was going on with in-store displays of plans and progress – all, of course, to the highest design standards.

The Malet Street/Gower Street building is an impressive gothic pile which extends over a whole block. The architect was Charles Fitzroy Doll and it was built in 1908. It was originally designed as a series of dwelling houses with shops on the ground-floor level; one of the key design issues was to convert this so that it appeared as a single entity; one very large but brilliant bookshop. As the design work started, regular formal weekly meetings were established between Fitch and Pentos executives and, most importantly, Dillon's staff. These were to continue during the building phase right up to the completion of the project. During the early stages our confused and sometimes contradictory ideas on what we were seeking to achieve were sifted and regurgitated by Fitch with Rodney playing a prominent role. The shop had to have authority, it would have a wider choice than any other bookshop, and that should be evident as people entered the store; it had to appear welcoming and friendly and *not* look like a library; it must not appear exclusive or élitist; it should be easy for customers to find their way around the five floors of bookshelves occupying 30,000 square feet of retail space and it should be made easier for them to find the books they wanted; it had to be elegant but (and Dillon's staff were rightly insistent on this) it also had to be practical; the shelving must be sufficiently flexible to be suitable for the wide range of book formats which now exist and to exploit fully the display potential of striking and well-designed book jackets. Fitch tried to reproduce all the thoughts on the usual designer's mood and story boards. Gradually it took shape: the now distinctive 'Dillons blue' and grey colour scheme; the dramatic open central staircase; acres of specially designed shelving units from Germany (but now manufactured in the UK by another Pentos company); a ground-floor store directory with more than one hundred subject headings with complementary signage throughout the store; eye-catching but eye-soothing green 'coolie' lights; 'Dillon's University Bookshop' to become the authoritative 'Dillons [no apostrophe!] the Bookstore' at Gower Street (more prominent than Malet Street to non-academics); and the introduction of a logo: a lower case gold 'd'.

When the presentations were made at the 'beauty parade' we had indicated a budget figure of £750,000 for the project but in the design discussions with Fitch it had become clear that this would need to be £1 million. This was the figure which we announced to the world at large when we told them of our plans and of the involvement of Fitch. There were elements within the book trade, particularly its trade press, which had long had doubts about my sanity. They were now convinced that I had finally taken leave of my senses. Nobody in Britain had ever spent a million pounds on a bookshop before; and this was a bookshop which already existed – not exactly a new shop. People are not going to buy more books just because the shop looks prettier, the doubters said. In fact the final cost was in excess of £1.5 million; and it should have been more – because we cut corners, which we later regretted, to keep costs down. It was the best single investment we ever made.

The shop was due to be re-opened formally (although it had never been entirely closed) by Princess Anne in September 1986. The work had been finished several days earlier, however, so that when the big day arrived we already had sufficient trading experience in the completed shop to know that it was a run-away success; sales were more than 40 per cent ahead of the same period in the previous year – and the shop was stunning. We had been excited when Princess Anne (now the Princess Royal) had agreed to perform the opening ceremony and to launch 'Dillons the Bookstore'. She was the Chancellor of the University of London and took a great interest in University affairs; she was also the member of the royal family I most admired. I was daunted, however, by the prospect of the protocol which it would involve. It is problematic enough dealing with the niceties of royal protocol (the 'sirs', 'ma'ams' and 'your royal highnesses') when a guest in the presence of royal personages; here I was to be the host and would therefore be by the side of Princess Anne throughout her entire visit to Dillons. I was to greet her as she left her car; escort her into the store; present to her those who had been most closely involved in the project and who would be standing in a long self-conscious line; make a short speech of welcome after which she would unveil a commemorative plaque; escort her through the shop where she would meet the staff; and then return her safely to her car. She arrived accompanied by her detectives and lady-in-waiting and was welcomed by an enthusiastic and noisy crowd who had gathered outside the store. She was brisk, businesslike, well-informed and appeared to take a genuine interest in what people had to say. She met all one hundred and fifty staff as she visited every part of the store and had a brief word with most of them. She asked Una Dillon, who was there as our special guest, what Una thought of the changes and was told that she did not like the new name – too American. Damned without even the hint of faint praise. Princess Anne stayed an hour longer than her scheduled time and left behind her the feeling of a great occasion. Even the most fervent republican, and there were many amongst the Gower Street staff, had been touched by her charm. I rushed home to see some brief footage of the visit on the television news and to change for the evening.

A celebratory dinner had been arranged at the Russell Hotel. It was not a hotel which would have been everybody's first choice for a grand, black tie, special occasion. However, the knowledgeable and knowing within the book trade had identified the connection. The architect of the Russell was the same Charles Fitzroy Doll who had designed the building which now housed Dillons in Gower Street. The truth of the matter was quite different. The chef at the Russell Hotel was Stefan Smolenski.

Stefan and I played football together every Sunday morning in Hyde Park. He was also a very good chef.

I had been persuaded that I should receive our guests as they arrived for dinner. As so often happens, a queue developed and people found themselves waiting at the back of a mounting crush without knowing quite what it was they were waiting for. I had until now kept myself relatively remote from book trade personalities and so I was meeting for the first time many of the publishers, literary agents, authors and journalists who were dining with us; which added to the delay. So the dinner got off to a late start. Service was then slow, the wine service sometimes non-existent, but the food was good – at least Stefan got it right. And the speeches were yet to come. I was to speak first and I was to introduce Una Dillon and also her sister Carmen, who was a distinguished theatre designer. Following me were Sir Peter Parker, who had become chairman of Dillon's when it was bought from Una by the University of London, Gordon Graham, who was the president of the Publishers' Association, John Mortimer and Sir Stephen Spender. By the time Stephen Spender rose to speak it was midnight. He was understandably brief but it was a lucid and literary end to a very special evening. It had been a long but momentous day; and it was to launch a programme which over the next seven years would mean an investment of more than £50 million and would establish Dillons as Britain's largest specialist bookseller and its leading and best-known brand. It was the start of a revolution in retail bookselling.

Dillons the Bookstore, as it was now known, had, for many years, been to its loyal but mainly academic customers Dillon's University Bookshop. It was now important to communicate to a wider market the existence of this centre of excellence. I have always maintained that it is the easiest thing in the world to sell books; the key is getting customers into the bookshop in the first place. We also needed to prepare the ground for a national chain of large stock-holding bookshops under the Dillons the Bookstore name. Dillons appointed an advertising agency, Leisure Advertising, which was led by an imaginative but practical ex-Saatchi executive, Paul Braithwaite. It was a relationship which was to last for the next eight years; a lifetime in the volatile and transient world of advertising. We had little money to spend and wanted to make as big an impact as possible on our modest budget; we hoped that the quality and provocative nature of the copy might create the added value of free editorial and news coverage in addition to the advertising space for which we had paid. We sought to develop a light, quirky style and a recognisable and consistent tone of voice. Amongst the first advertisements was one which enquired: 'Foiled again? Try Dillons.' It made play of Foyle's often non-English-speaking assistants' notorious inability to locate books within its extensive shelves. We used the copy on posters as well as in newspaper advertising and one of the posters was placed at a bus-stop in the Charing Cross Road immediately outside Foyle's main entrance. The hoped-for news coverage followed and within London our small campaign was soon a talking point. Copy for other advertisements included 'Browsers Welcome (high brows and low brows)' and 'Where to pick up what you can't put down'; they all featured the same distinctive layout and typeface which became identified with Dillons. In the first three years with Leisure Advertising Dillons' total spend on advertising, including a number of regional launches for new or refurbished shops, was less than £750,000. The high-profile and highly effective London poster campaign cost £60,000. All this was small beer by advertising trade standards, but, at that time, a fortune in the context of a marketing-illiterate book trade. Paul Braithwaite and his team provided the advertising support in the subsequent 'lower book prices' promotions which Dillons launched as part of its campaign for the abolition of the net book agreement. Once Reed had left the net book agreement in 1991 it was possible to develop harder and more focused copy, and the digs in later copylines were a little less gentle: 'David Lodge's new novel must be good. W.H. Smith are charging £3.79 more for it' was one of them.

Advertising played a crucial role in helping to establish the Dillons brand. Window displays were also important, and Dillons was fortunate in having Mandy Walker, a person of great flair and creativity, in charge of the in-house design team which was responsible for window and in-store and point of sale display. We gave a high priority to presenting the promise of the store through attractive and stimulating windows; and Mandy's dramatic and eye-catching montages, which she would proudly present to me at a personal preview, were amongst the best in London.

It is useful to look in a little more detail at the figures in assessing the remarkable success of the Gower Street re-launch. Sales from the shop at the time of its acquisition in 1977 had been £2.5 million; they were £6.5 million in 1985, the year before the refurbishment. At a time of high inflation, sales had increased a little ahead of the increase in prices. In 1987, the first full year after the re-fit, they were £11.5 million, an increase of 75 per cent in two years and in real terms, allowing for price increases, the equivalent of more than an extra 60 per cent in numbers of books sold. Retail selling space had increased from 22,000 square feet to 30,000 square feet, spread over five floors, an increase of 36 per cent, and 250,000 different titles were now carried in stock. Sales have continued to grow rapidly, and today sales are running at about £20 million a year generated from a stockholding at retail values of around £5 million; profits at store level are between £2.5 million and £3 million. Sales from this one shop are equivalent to 1½ per cent of total UK retail book sales from the whole trade and by any measure of performance the store compares favourably with almost any other area of retail activity; it probably has higher sales and higher profits than any other bookshop in the world.

At the beginning of 1987, with the confidence drawn from the Gower Street success, a decision was taken to re-fit, with two exceptions, all the Pentos-owned bookshops to the Fitch design concept and to rebadge them as Dillons the Bookstore; at that time most were called Hudsons. The two exceptions were Hodges Figgis and the Athena bookshops. Hodges Figgis was a Dublin-based bookshop with a distinguished and long history; it would not benefit from the national 'brand' advertising planned for the UK media, and there was, therefore, no point in changing Hodges Figgis's well-known name. Later Hodges Figgis was to be re-sited to a much larger and improved position in Dawson Street and the new shop was built to a modified Fitch design ('Hodges Figgis green' rather than 'Dillons blue'); it is now the largest and most successful bookshop in Ireland.

We had developed the Athena bookshop concept in 1984 in partnership with the designer Jon Isherwood; I was very much involved with the original idea (as was Frank Brazier) and I had personally identified the location for the first shop in Coventry Street when hobbling around shopping developments in central London one weekend with my right leg in plaster, having returned from a foreshortened holiday with a skiing injury. The concept was born out of our frustration at our inability to widen sufficiently the appeal of our more conventional bookshops (which was pre-Fitch). We wanted to find new ways of getting new people – particularly young people – into bookshops; we had in mind that well-used trade statistic that 50 per cent of the people in Britain never visit a bookshop in their lives. We had already, again with Jon Isherwood, successfully updated the Athena galleries, which in a high-fashion environment were now selling large quantities of posters, cards and prints to a youngish market. The new idea was to extend the Athena concept from the one thousand square feet gallery size to a sales area of around five thousand square feet, with the additional space being devoted to the sale of books displayed in the same stylish environment. These we named Athena bookshops. They were up-beat; used light and colour and sound (pop music and jazz) to create an air of excitement; they appealed to a younger age group across a far broader cross-section of society; and they sold large quantities of a surprisingly wide range of books. The original Athena bookshop in Coventry Street, as an example, is open 364 days a year until eleven o'clock each evening; its busiest hour is often between ten and eleven at night – selling thousands of books which would not otherwise have been sold. Over the next three years we opened thirteen Athena bookshops, all in prime locations, and they, particularly the earlier ones, were very successful. Sadly, they were overtaken by Dillons. Dillons' new stores were capital-hungry and obsessive in their demands on senior management time. The validity of the original concept for the Athena bookshops was now in doubt; they became neglected and lacked direction and leadership (they were managed quite separately from the Athena galleries); after

1988 no new shops were opened and the performance of the existing shops deteriorated; they undeservedly paid the price for the greater success of Dillons.

In addition to the branding of the existing bookshops as Dillons Bookstores, we were now looking a little more aggressively at opportunities to acquire existing bookshops and to open new ones to add to what was now a Dillons chain. Late in 1986, we had acquired the Arts Council Bookshop in Long Acre; it was the outcome of the most astonishing story of muddle and indecisiveness. We had been informed by the Arts Council that it wished to sell its bookshop and, together with Dillons' then development director Don Noble, I attended a meeting of its relevant sub-committee to present our credentials. We made an offer to buy the lease for £50,000 and to pay for the stock on an agreed basis of valuation. We were disappointed when we were told that our offer had been unsuccessful and that the shop was to be purchased by Waterstone's; this news eventually appeared in the trade press together with details of its staffing for which new booksellers were being recruited. There was then a period of silence which continued for rather longer than would normally be expected. It was broken when I received a call from the Arts Council in which I was told, to its obvious embarrassment, that the sale to Waterstone's could not go ahead as the Waterstone covenant (this was before the group's acquisition by W.H. Smith) was not acceptable to the institutional landlord of the shop's premises; I was told that, if Dillons still wished to proceed, the shop was ours. I confirmed that our offer still stood, but I was insistent that any acceptance of our offer must be unconditional so that, for example, it would not be possible for Waterstone's to renew its offer should it find some way of rectifying its flawed covenant; there must be no room for 'gazumping'. This was agreed, and Dillons' solicitors were instructed to proceed. Some weeks later, within days of the agreed date for the completion of the purchase, I received a call from a distressed Frank Brazier; he told me that Don Noble had been informed by the Arts Council that Waterstone's had been able to resolve its lease problems with the landlord, and, as theirs was a better offer, the Dillons deal was off. We were very angry, as this was a possibility which we had anticipated and on which we had been given assurances; when dealing with property matters there are certain people on whose word it would be unwise to rely, but we had not thought that this could possibly apply to the Arts Council. Frank Brazier's view was that there was nothing more which we could now do, but I was determined not to leave it there. The following morning, as it seemed we had nothing more to lose, I drafted the strongest possible letter to the Chairman of the Arts Council who was then Sir William Rees-Mogg (now Lord Rees-Mogg) and who was clearly unaware of what was being done. I set out the sequence of events and described the behaviour as totally unacceptable. The letter was delivered by hand at ten o'clock, and, as this was not the time to pull punches, I threatened to call a press conference to expose the shabby episode if I did not receive a satisfactory response by midday. At eleven I received a telephone call; the shop was ours. Some three years later Lord Rees-Mogg added a postscript when writing to me on another matter: 'I should like to congratulate you on the excellent arts bookshop in Long Acre. I remember there was some difficulty about the sale and we nearly sold the bookshop to two people at the same time, so I am particularly glad that it all worked out well in the end.'

The first entirely new bookshop opened in the new

Fitch/Dillons design concept was in Oxford in 1987. Debenhams were trading from prominent Oxford premises as a department store and we had been told that the property was on the market. It occupied a corner site at the junction of Cornmarket and Broad Street; it was close to the academic heartland, being at the opposite end of Broad Street to Blackwells (the occupying bookselling force which enjoyed a virtual monopoly in Oxford), whilst also being part of the high street retailing scene, which Blackwells was not. It could not have been better located for a bookshop, particularly for the kind of bookselling in which Dillons believed, and I was determined that we should get it. After some initial uncertainty, Jim Clark, our property director, was able to telephone me from Burton's (Debenhams' owners) offices in Leeds to say that our offer had been accepted. We set to work to design and build the largest new bookshop ever opened in the UK; it was to set the pattern for the future. The project was always going to be a major undertaking, but we needlessly made it far more complicated by seeking to introduce a new electronic point-of-sale system at the same time. We hired a separate warehouse to receive the initial stock of books from publishers and printed our own bar code labels, which then had to be placed on the books; the system was unbelievably time-consuming and was aborted shortly after the shop opened (it was to be resurrected the following year, and Dillons' early commitment to EPOS was to pay handsome dividends). Despite this delay, the shop was opened on time by Lord Jenkins, Oxford's Chancellor; it had cost one and a half million pounds and we had created 13,000 square feet of retail space from which book sales in its first year were more than three million pounds – they are currently around six million. Once again there had been the usual sceptics in the book trade: 'Oxford already has a bookshop,' they said, as if one bookshop was enough and competition in bookselling something to be avoided; they hardly seemed to notice that Oxford had several wine shops – to mention just one other area of retailing – and all seemed to prosper. In fact the new bookshop has been good for Oxford, bookbuyers have choice; good for Dillons, it has been a highly profitable bookshop; good for Blackwells, because, I believe, the competition has kept them on their toes; and good for the book trade, because many more books are now being sold in Oxford – Blackwells' sales were not reduced by the value of Dillons' sales.

In 1988, Dillons opened in Cambridge; which, in its turn, became, at 15,000 square feet, the largest new bookshop to be opened in the UK. Cambridge has traded well but it has never quite matched the performance of Oxford; and the response of Heffers (the resident Cambridge bookshop) to this new competition was perhaps a little more spirited than that of Blackwells. Another highlight of 1988 was the acquisition of Mowbrays, a long-established bookshop in Margaret Street, London, with a strong reputation for religious books and which has since been refitted and renamed Dillons.

In 1989, the pace quickened. New, large Dillons Bookstores were opened in Dublin (Hodges Figgis), Aberdeen, Cardiff, Leicester, Newcastle, Southampton and Exeter. Dillons also purchased H.K. Lewis, a distinguished medical bookseller, and integrated it with the medical department of the Gower Street store to create the largest medical bookshop in the country. The cost of creating this new space was high. A typical new Dillons Bookstore was between 10,000 and 15,000 square feet. To fit out to the very high standards which Dillons had established, usually including a dramatic central staircase to provide easy access to the several trading floors, cost £100 per square foot. The stockholding at retail values was at least a further £100 per square foot, so that the total investment in a new store could be between two and two and a half million pounds. At the end of 1989 we paused for breath; sales in the year had increased by 34 per cent and were now running at an annual rate of around £70 million; we were trading from 61 bookshops and 300,000 square feet of retailing space; but the storm clouds of recession were gathering, and, although this would create more property opportunities and enable us to open further new stores on better terms, the trading outlook was clearly deteriorating.

On May 10, 1989, I took a telephone call from Tim Waterstone. He needed to see me urgently and we agreed to meet in my office at a quarter to nine the following morning. Waterstone's was Dillons' only serious competition. Tim Waterstone had started the eponymous bookshop chain a few years earlier with venture capital support. He and I had both been pursuing aggressive expansion programmes and we were often bidding against each other to be in the same locations. Dillons' rate of growth had been greater in the past two years and the Dillons chain was bigger and geographically more widely spread, whilst the Waterstone chain, at that time, was concentrated very much in London; but there was no question that Waterstone's was the competitor to watch. Tim Waterstone is a likeable fellow; he has an endearing, panglossian approach to the book trade: everything is for the best in this best of all possible book worlds, so why change anything; he spoke of the net book agreement with the natural fervour of the convert – which he was. In many ways we shared a common approach to book retailing; a belief in large, well-stocked bookshops, staffed by knowledgeable and helpful booksellers, offering a wide range of choice in a congenial ambience, and with a high degree of devolution to individual shop managers. But there were important differences. Waterstone's aimed for a more literary market and its shops sought a more literary feel; and, as Tim Waterstone was quoted as saying in *Marketing Week*: 'We never set out to broaden the book market, but we do an excellent job of getting those who do buy books to buy more of them.' Dillons' objective was the more difficult one of 'widening the market for books'. Dillons stores were designed to be welcoming and to break down the traditional resistance on the part of many, if not most, people to crossing the threshold of a specialist bookshop; they were meant to be an integral part of the modern retailing scene; nonetheless, they were serious bookshops covering the whole spectrum of subject areas with strong academic departments as well as the broadest range of literary and general titles; a typical Dillons would stock 70,000 different titles (at Gower Street it was 250,000 titles) and would aim to meet all the requirements of the bookbuyer, bringing one-stop shopping to book retailing – what the Americans would inelegantly call a category killer. This meant that Dillons' new stores were usually larger than Waterstone's and in 1990 it was thought that, of the fifteen largest UK bookshops, eleven were owned by Dillons – each of the remaining four belonging to a different owner.

Tim arrived for our morning meeting looking as if he had not slept; he was tense and drawn and depressed. He explained that he was looking for a buyer for Waterstone's; there had been earlier re-financings from his existing and new backers but he had again run out of money. He did not have the resources to satisfy the needs of the shops already opened, let alone to provide the funds required to open the new shops to which he was committed; and the trading record would not support the option of going back to the City for more cash. He showed me the figures. The business was still failing to make money but Tim laid great stress on the relative immaturity of the recently opened shops (a concept with which I was more than familiar) and produced projections which showed aggressive profits growth as the shops became established. I was a little sceptical about the figures but the acquisition of Waterstone's by Dillons would be of great strategic value. Waterstone's and Dillons were often competing for new shops and prospective landlords were not slow to exploit the possibilities in playing one off against the other. The problem was how to make sense of the numbers.

Waterstone's owed the banks around £10 million and had capital commitments to open new shops which I estimated would cost another £5 million. So where was the value for the equity? It was difficult to see how the shareholders' interests had any great value at all. Nonetheless, I suggested to Tim, very tentatively, but in the hope of keeping the dialogue open, that, assuming his figures could be verified, Dillons might be able to stretch to £15 million to acquire the whole of the share capital of Waterstone's. As Dillons would then have to assume responsibility for the bank debt and for the financing of the unopened shops, this would have meant a total investment of £30 million. On the basis of my existing knowledge of the business, and of the information which Tim had given to me, this could not, I believed, be justified and I assumed that in later negotiations and after any subsequent due diligence investigations there would need to be some downwards adjustment. Tim left my office in despondent mood, but with the clear understanding that Dillons had an interest in acquiring his business and that our preliminary indications would value it at £15 million. I heard and saw nothing of Tim for a while, and, as the weeks turned into months, the gossip in the trade was that Smith's was to buy Waterstone's. There was a sighting of Tim with Malcolm Field at some Scottish airport, apparently on a tour of the Waterstone's shops, and then, in August, came the announcement: Smith's had agreed to acquire Waterstone's on a complicated formula but which meant it was to pay around £43 million for the equity; taking into account the added burden of the bank debt and the need to fund the shops still to be opened, it meant a total investment by Smith's of almost £60 million. It was a staggering sum to pay for a business yet to make a profit and with annual sales at that time of less than £40 million. It seemed to me that, strategically, Smith's was absolutely right to buy Waterstone's. Smith's had been negligent in leaving the field to Dillons and Waterstone's to exploit the market opportunity for large, attractive specialist bookshops. Its own specialist bookselling chain, Sherratt and Hughes, was tired and lacklustre. But why on earth had it paid so much? Dillons had suggested a figure little more than one-third of that which Smith's was now paying and Waterstone's had nowhere else to go. What a price it was now paying for its earlier failure.

Tim Waterstone, of course, had done a fabulous deal. It supported my long-held belief that entrepreneurs most often make most money from the timing and execution of financial transactions with well-targeted, deal-hungry purchasers, rather than in the painstaking, high-risk process of building a business for the longer term. A good slice of luck also helps. Within the book trade, perhaps the best example of this phenomenon is Paul Hamlyn, who has twice capitalised on his undoubted business success by exiting with well-timed and well-executed deals with a buyer who had been identified as having a unique strategic interest in making the acquisition. Anthony Cheetham also made the most of the less obviously commercially successful Century Hutchinson in selling to the then managerially strapped but acquisition-driven American publishing company Random House.

Another diversion from the more routine day-to-day activities in 1989 was provided by Robert Maxwell. Around the middle of the year, I became aware that we were having supply problems with Macdonald's, the book publisher owned by the Maxwell interests. It is not entirely unknown for a bookseller and publisher to be in dispute about timely payment for goods supplied, and the threat of a suspension of supplies is a very powerful weapon to ensure prompt payment. However, the problem with Macdonald's appeared to be more complicated that this. Payments on the account were being made according to terms which had been agreed, but outstanding orders were still not being released. Indeed, we reached the farcical situation where, as subsequent payments were made as they fell due and as there were no new purchases, the outstanding balance rapidly approached zero – yet still we could not get supplies. Macdonald's executives were highly embarrassed in trying to explain the situation to Dillons. Mr Maxwell, they said, was very unhappy with the Dillons account; but they could not establish what it was we had to do to correct whatever it was that was wrong. Then it was put to us that supplies would be resumed if we would agree to a unilateral and onerous change in our trading terms. This we flatly refused to do, and we had to reconcile ourselves to obtaining Macdonald titles from wholesalers, although this was not always possible. Which was where the matter rested when I received a telephone call at home on a Sunday early in August from Robert Peston, a journalist on the *Independent*. I knew Peston reasonably well and had a high regard for him. He told me that he understood that Dillons were 'on stop' with Macdonald's (and therefore receiving no books from them) on instructions from Robert Maxwell because of our failure to pay the account, and asked for my comments. The issue of Dillons' alleged disputes with publishers was a hardy annual and the reports – usually misinformed – were damaging to the reputation of Dillons and of Pentos. I was able to say to Robert Peston, with accuracy, that far from being behind in paying our account with Maxwell, 'we do not owe him one cent'. We speculated on what could be the reason for Maxwell's obduracy. We lighted on the unflattering biography *Maxwell the Outsider* by Tom Bower which had so incensed Maxwell. Dillons, along with other booksellers, had received writs for defamation and these had been followed up by the most aggressive letters in typical Maxwell fashion. Despite this Dillons, in accordance with its general policy with regard to any attempt to impose censorship, had kept the book on sale, albeit with the slight comfort of an indemnity from the publisher. It now turned out that other booksellers had in fact withdrawn the book from sale, and that Dillons was standing virtually alone. Robert Peston allowed this speculation to spill over into his article the following day; the full fury of Maxwell was to follow. I received a ferocious letter signed by one of the Maxwell sons but in the poisonous style of the father. I spoke to Peter Jay, who was then Maxwell's aide-de-camp, in the hope of bringing some sanity into the situation, but in vain. He was icily cold, unfriendly, unhelpful, detached. The inevitable writs followed: one for me, one for Robert Peston and one for Andreas Whittam-Smith, the editor of the *Independent*. The writs were for defamation, although my lawyers advised me I was the person who had been defamed. Nonetheless, the sensible thing to do was to see if there was an acceptable basis for a settlement as legal disputes with Maxwell were always costly, time-consuming and counter-productive. About one thing I was adamant, however. I was not going to offer the apology requested as I had absolutely nothing for which to apologise. Victor Blank offered to mediate with Maxwell as he knew him slightly. He returned from his meeting on noticeably more friendly personal terms with Maxwell but it was not obvious that he had progressed our cause. Lawyers consulted. We reluctantly agreed to pay the most nominal sum to a Maxwell-favoured charity and to pay his costs. Trading relationships with Dillons were re-established on the terms which had existed prior to the dispute; there was no apology – and we continued to sell the Tom Bower book. As it so happened, before we were required to settle the costs issue, Maxwell went for the long swim from which he was not to return.

A major strategic move was made by Dillons in 1990 with the acquisition of Hatchards. William Collins, the publisher, had been the owner of Hatchards since 1957, and Ian Chapman, Collins' former chairman, had a strong emotional attachment to it; my several approaches in recent years had always met with a friendly but firm refusal. However, Collins had been acquired by News International in 1989 and it did not have the same commitment to book retailing.

The history of Hatchards dates back to 1797, when the original Hatchards bookstore was opened in Piccadilly by

John Hatchard. There has been a Hatchards bookstore in Piccadilly ever since and it is one of only twelve companies to have been awarded all four royal warrants; it also enjoyed an international reputation and was second only to Foyle's as a bookshop destination for overseas visitors. In recent years there had been a number of new store openings in a late, half-hearted and unsuccessful attempt to compete with the developing Dillons and Waterstone's chains – their new shops were much smaller, typically 3,000 square feet. It had also acquired in 1986 Claude Gill, another small chain of bookshops. By 1990, therefore, Hatchards owned 26 bookshops in total, traded from 100,000 square feet of retail space, and had annual sales of more than £25 million; with about 2.5 per cent of the total retail book market, it was ranked number four of the *specialist* booksellers behind Dillons, Waterstone's and Blackwells (although, of course, W.H. Smith remained the dominant book retailer). Dillons paid £10.5 million for Hatchards and it was a quantum leap in terms of Dillons' strength and influence within the book trade. Dillons (including Hatchards) now had a 10 per cent share of the retail book market; in London it accounted for as much as 30 per cent of total book sales; and Hatchards at Piccadilly sold more copies of new hardback fiction than any other bookshop in the country. The Hatchards acquisition meant that, in a period of twelve months, there had been a significant change in the structure of the retail book trade in Britain. A year earlier there had been four specialist booksellers with ambitions to build national chains: Dillons and Waterstone's, the pace-setters; Sherratt and Hughes, the Smith's subsidiary, which would surely have got its act together eventually; and Hatchards. Now there were only two. It represented a dramatic improvement in Dillons' strategic position in bookselling.

Royal warrants are held by an individual rather than a company, and the four warrants which Hatchards held were in the name of Peter Giddy, its long-standing director and general manager. We now had to go through the process of seeking the approval of the grantors to the transfer of the warrants from his name to mine; the warrants were shortly reissued to me, and I found myself, nominally, the appointed bookseller to the Queen, the Queen Mother, the Duke of Edinburgh and the Prince of Wales – something which would certainly not have featured in any career plan of mine in those earlier years. When the announcement came from the Lord Chamberlain's office, the strongly anti-Dillons trade publication, the *Bookseller*, was moved to write, 'Even those booksellers who detest Mr Maher's stance on the net book agreement will concur – however grudgingly – that the new bookseller to the royal family has done more for the quality of bookshops in this country than anyone else in the last decade and he will almost certainly turn Hatchards into a shop fit to hold the royal warrants which it had ceased to be under its previous owner.'

The first task, after the acquisition, was to refit the Piccadilly store. Of the twenty-five Hatchards and Claude Gill shops which represented the branch network, most were to be re-badged – and in many cases refurbished – as Dillons Bookstores, although some of the smaller and less well situated shops were to be closed. The flagship store in Piccadilly, however, which for most people *was* Hatchards, was to retain its name and was to be substantially rebuilt and refitted. The present premises had been occupied for more than one hundred years and it showed. There had been little new investment in the shop in recent times, and, although it retained its authentic charm, the neglect had resulted in a very down-at-heel appearance

– very much like the newly impoverished gentry who represented such an important part of its customer base. Fitch was called in again, and Rodney did his usual magic. The key part of the brief was that this was *not* a Dillons; we must at all costs retain the essential character of Hatchards. We had to bring the shop into the almost twenty-first century without it being obvious; at the same time we must create much more space for books and make it a more efficient store for both the customers and staff. The shop quickly became a building site and the project a nightmare; clearly nineteenth-century building regulations did not provide for basic matters such as foundations. As we dug down to provide more headroom in basement areas which were to be converted to retail space we found that the shop had almost literally been built on shifting sands; we had to prop up the walls and lay the foundations which the buildings had never had – I half-expected to arrive one morning to find a gaping hole in the middle of Piccadilly where our shop had once stood. As we broke through each wall, we were never sure what we would find on the other side; the usual plans and architect's drawings, which normally provide the clues, did not exist. Gradually, however, the new shop took shape – at the inevitable additional cost of time and money. Hatchards held a headlease on the main Piccadilly premises at a peppercorn rent and a refinancing of this lease provided the funds for the rebuilding and also for the refurbishment of some of the other, smaller Hatchards and Claude Gill shops.

I was receiving letters from many parts of the world from customers who were concerned that I was destroying part of our national heritage. And I was told that Dirk Bogarde was so appalled at the apparent vandalism that he vowed never to visit the shop again (he has since spent many – I hope, happy – hours signing books in the new store). Concern at the demolition of a staircase thought to be of great antiquity was assuaged when it was explained that it dated in fact from the 1950s, and the very old fireplaces which anxious observers saw being taken away were simply going to specialists to be restored, then returned and refitted. People need not have been concerned; Fitch was so successful in retaining the feel and appearance of the old store that *Private Eye* was able to write that I had spent £2.5 million on making Hatchards look the same, but more downmarket – which was more than a little unfair, but for *Private Eye* quite mild. When the shop reopened, we had created 30 per cent more retail space but, critically, 70 per cent more shelf space; we were therefore able to widen the range of stock carried to 100,000 titles and to display the books far more effectively. The sales pattern was distorted by the increasing impact of the recession, which was particularly hard on consumer spending in central London, and by the reduction in the number of overseas visitors to the UK. Nonetheless, sales volumes eventually settled at levels significantly higher than those which existed prior to the refit and it reversed a downward trend which had been established for several years; the shop now trades from five floors and 12,000 square feet of retail space and achieves a productivity level of more than £500 per square foot. The size of my postbag increased again; but this time it was with compliments and not a single critical comment that I can remember; and Hatchards has become for me personally a very special shop.

The Hatchards acquisition did not impede the continuing roll-out of the Dillons chain – and, as predicted, a silver lining within the clouds of the deepening recession was reduced competition for new space and the ability to acquire it on more favourable terms. In 1990, seven new large stores were opened including Coventry and Belfast, and, in central London, the Kings Road and Kensington High Street. The Kensington shop was an enormous 16,500 square feet, and took over from Cambridge the mantle of the biggest new bookshop in Britain. We had, from the outset, a number of reservations about the position of the shop: it was on the 'wrong' side of the High Street, and it had an exceptionally narrow frontage relative to the overall size of the store. We employed Management Horizons to do some independent research, and we put more homework into the analysis of its prospects than for any other shop which I can remember. The conclusion was that the immediate footfall, and the estimated size of the available book market within its catchment area (allowing for existing competition), was more than enough to justify the investment. We went ahead and created a store of great visual impact – once a customer was inside the shop; but there were insufficient customers (since the opening of the store, a pedestrian barrier had been built by the local authority which made access across the busy High Street even more difficult) and we would have been wiser to have followed our first instincts. It was a mistake; it was the first of our new large Dillons Bookstores to be a failure.

In 1991, we opened in Manchester, Watford, Hatfield, Leeds, Southampton and Trafalgar Square. We also acquired the Economist Bookshops, a small chain of six shops which included the Clare Market bookshop, which has close links with the London School of Economics. The 1991 new openings were a mixed bag. Watford and Leeds have yet to establish themselves as successful bookshops; Hatfield, after a brilliant first year, has since slowed down due to problems at the shopping centre in which it is situated, but there is no reason why it should not recover once those problems have been resolved; Southampton was a success; and Manchester and Trafalgar Square were outstanding. The Manchester opening was particularly satisfying as the store is situated in St Anne's Square directly opposite the bookshop which I had first entered as a boy with such trepidation; and the Trafalgar Square shop was especially pleasing because Dillons was established from the outset as a successful destination store in a new development (Grand Buildings) which was not a traditional or obvious retail pitch, and which had no adjacent attractions, retail or otherwise – it was an excellent example of the pulling power of Dillons and of the kind of bookselling in which it believes.

At the end of 1991, Dillons was trading from 105 bookshops and 500,000 square feet of space and sales were running at an annual rate of £125 million. This represented a 65 per cent increase in space and a 75 per cent increase in sales in just two years. The winds of recession were now of gale force, however, and it was difficult to improve profitability. The recession had particularly hit consumer spending, and, therefore, retailers. Despite this, Dillons' underlying sales performance remained relatively strong; on a strict like-for-like comparison for those shops which had been open for the whole of each year (the best measure of relative performance), Dillons' sales increases were 10 per cent in 1990 and 5.5 per cent in 1991 – which was better than retailers' overall performance and better than any other bookselling chain. The problem, however, was that occupancy costs were rising at a faster rate than sales; a combination of the newly established uniform business rate and the unrelenting, ratchet-like impact of upwards-only rent reviews. Dillons had weathered this recession better than most retailers, but the pressures were building up.

There had never been a love affair between booksellers and business systems. Whereas other retailers had recognised the opportunities for stock control and sophisticated marketing techniques, and had played an important part in the evolution of business machines into the full-blown electronic point-of-sale systems which are commonplace today, booksellers had stayed in the ark. Until very recently, a typical bookseller controlled his stock through a card index system. He might check the physical stock of a particular title against the stock card each month, although too often if he was busy, or understaffed, or just could not be bothered, this could easily stretch to two or three months – or longer. He would only then discover how many copies had been sold – or stolen – and if appropriate generate a re-order. Often this routine would be short-circuited when a customer found that a particular title was out of stock; the book would then be specially ordered – although many customers would not be prepared to wait the two weeks they would usually be told it would take. This was the system which, for example, operated at Gower Street and at Hudsons in Birmingham. Although booksellers had been left behind in the move to electronic retailing, it was bookshops which had most to gain from improved systems. There are 60,000 to 70,000 new titles (new products to other retailers) published each year; there are around 500,000 titles currently in print. No other retail business has such diversity; so many different product lines. Yet the key to successful bookselling is the range and quality of the stock; dead stock needs to be identified quickly and returned to the publisher, and the bookseller needs to know which titles are selling so that they can speedily be replenished. So systems which give the bookseller the information he needs to take these decisions on a regular daily basis are absolutely critical.

Dillons had been developing an electronic point-of-sale (EPOS) system since before 1987. We were having to leapfrog all the intermediate stages of development which, over many years, other retail businesses had gone through, and having to move directly from manual systems to state-of-the-art electronic systems. Standard packages were being developed by a number of computer software houses and these were soon being peddled around the book trade; but, whilst suitable for smaller bookshops which might carry 20,000 titles in stock, they were not appropriate for the typical new Dillons store which would have up to 70,000 titles in stock, let alone Gower Street where the stockholding was 250,000 titles. Dillons, therefore, again had no alternative to being an ambitious pioneer. After the initial abortive exercise in 1987, an EPOS system developed by Dillons working with a software house was successfully introduced in Oxford in 1988. This system and a modified version were subsequently introduced into all the new Dillons Bookstores and over the next three years into the larger existing stores including, most importantly, Gower Street in 1991.

The EPOS system improves stock control by enabling booksellers to return slow-moving stock and to re-order fast-moving stock more quickly; it improves customer service by making it more likely that the required book will be in stock and by providing up-to-the-minute, touch-of-the-finger information on stock availability (typically, 40 per cent of customers entering a bookshop to purchase a specific title will leave disappointed as the book is out of stock); and it enables the marketing department to plan more focused promotions and to have immediate feedback of sales data on promotions currently running (this will obviously be of dramatically greater value with the promotional opportunities which will exist once the net book agreement has been abolished). It has also enabled Dillons to develop a core stocklist of over 12,000 titles, which in most stores have to be carried in stock at all times.

EPOS systems now exist in all major Dillons stores and capture information on more than 80 per cent of total sales by value; but much still needs to be done. The acquisition of Hatchards brought with it EPOS systems which were more limited in scope and these need to be upgraded to the more advanced specifications of the Dillons system so that a single system operates within the expanded chain; the EPOS system is not yet integrated with the head office accounting system, which continues to be antiquated; the potential for automatic re-ordering of books from publishers which exists within the present system needs to be realised; and the labour-intensive nature of processing incoming deliveries onto the system needs to be improved. However, the major pioneering work has been done and much of the investment in hardware and in software has been incurred, although there will be a further sizeable investment when the head office systems are brought into line. The tangible rewards of better stock control, improved customer service and more focused marketing have only recently begun to be realised but they make an essential project also a profitable one.

A number of publishers believed that they were the people who were financing Dillons' investment programme. If only it had been so. An annual event, usually in the summer 'silly' season, was a flurry of trade press comment that 'Dillons don't pay their bills';

and in the gossipy world of the book trade there was always a publisher or two who could be relied upon for a quote. What they were really saying of course was that Dillons were not paying as quickly as the publisher would like, but this was not always made clear. I have no doubt that there were occasions, more than I would like, when Dillons were slow in settling suppliers' accounts; but this was invariably due to the antiquated, manual head office systems, which had failed to keep pace with Dillons' expansion rather than a deliberate act of policy (policies might well have changed, however, during the past year). Unfortunately, it would usually be the smaller, more vulnerable, publisher who suffered from delay in this paperchase. Dillons deals with 7,000 different suppliers, but just 200 of them account for 80 per cent by value of Dillons' purchases, and these large publishers had a fixed agreed payment date each month. So it was rare, but not unknown, for there to be a dispute with a major supplier, although the smaller publishers often had a legitimate case for complaint. However, there was never, at any time, and quite unlike the practice in many other retail businesses, the slightest risk of trade credit being used to finance new shop openings. Dillons aimed for, and just failed to reach, a stock turn of three; in other words an average book took four months to sell. By normal retailing standards this was a low stock turn, albeit better than that achieved by other specialist booksellers; a low stock turn is the price paid for range – although range also has its own reward in terms of higher overall sales. Dillons typically paid the publisher for a book three months after the invoice date; a book purchased in January would normally be paid for in the first two weeks of April. Some accounts would be settled earlier, and some later, but that was the average. So, if it takes four months to sell a book, and it has been paid for in three months, then the supplier is financing 75 per cent of the investment in stock and the retailer 25 per cent. In practice, Dillons' experience was that trade creditor finance rarely rose above 70 per cent; the publisher, far from helping to finance the capital costs of the new shops, was not even fully funding the stockholding; which will astonish those involved in the faster-moving sectors of the retail trade.

In 1992, large new Dillons Bookstores were opened in Glasgow, Kingston, Crawley, Thurrock and Darlington. All performed in line with expectations with Kingston as the star. Like-for-like sales increases from existing shops were 4 per cent, which although Dillons' most disappointing performance so far, was still a figure which was better than that being achieved by most other retailers.

1993 was to see, at last, the end of the recession; it also marked the final stages of Dillons' explosive dash for growth. The end of the chapter for me was the opening of the new Dillons in central Birmingham in August 1993, although further new shops were still to be opened in Aylesbury, Sutton and Plymouth later in the year.

The former headquarters building of the Midland Bank had become available in 1991 and Dillons in partnership with a local developer had agreed terms to take it over and to convert it into a bookshop. The lease on the existing Dillons shop in Birmingham (which had been the original Hudsons bookshop) was soon to expire and we had been looking with increasing desperation for a new shop, so that the availability of the Midland Bank building was timely. It was situated by Birmingham's New Street railway station and could not have been better placed. It was an imposing, Grade II-listed, Victorian building dating back to 1865. Like so many of the new

Dillons Bookstores, the building was of great architectural interest but many of the most spectacular architectural features had been covered up long ago and much of the early building work was in the nature of exploration and in unveiling its hidden secrets. As Rodney Fitch remarked to me, 'We are really in the business of recycling historic buildings': we were finding a new role for them which was relevant to today's needs. This was the most ambitious project yet. One of the most beautiful features of the building was a stained-glass domed ceiling which had been blacked out and lost to the public view probably during the 1930s or 1940s. Each of the delicate glass dome panels was cleaned and restored and the dome was then dramatically repositioned to a height some fifty feet above the ground floor; it was raised literally to the roof, from where it now casts down natural light to the lower levels of the store. It cost £4.5 million to build the store, of which £2 million was paid by the developer and £2.5 million by Dillons. We created 20,000 square feet of retailing space, making it second in size only to Gower Street; it also became the second largest shop in terms of sales at £7.5 million per annum (in line with expectations), overtaking Oxford and Piccadilly. But the most satisfying feature is its breathtaking beauty; of the many attractive stores which we have opened over the past six years, it is, aesthetically, easily the most pleasing. And the manager happens to be my middle son, Anthony.

In developing the Dillons chain in the late Eighties and early Nineties, Pentos had taken advantage of a unique opportunity to build a high-quality retail business for the longer-term benefit of its shareholders. If there was a mistake, it was the important one of not communicating this message sufficiently clearly to the stock market. The City, which has long been accused of short-termism, has become even more obsessively concerned with short-term performance in recent years; and it is unforgiving with regard to any failure to meet its short-term expectations. We might have been wiser to have spelt out in more detail the nature of the enterprise on which we were embarked; to have dampened, deliberately, immediate profit expectations, whilst pointing to the powerful, strategic position which was being established within the book trade. It is always better to promise little and deliver more, but the reality is often the reverse. Perhaps, also, we had assumed a degree of sophistication in the stock market which is not justified; we believed that it would share our vision and value it accordingly; and we were wrong.

The Dillons business has grown from the £4 million annual turnover being achieved by Dillon's University Bookshops in 1977 to today's £150 million sales by Dillons Bookstores; in the last five years alone, sales have trebled at a time of the fiercest recession any of us can remember. There are now more than one hundred Dillons shops throughout the country, and their sales account for 12 per cent of the total UK retail book market. Dillons is the second largest book retailer (only the combined sales of W.H. Smith and its subsidiary Waterstone's are greater), is the largest of the specialist booksellers, and (so says independent research) is the country's best-known and highest-regarded book chain. It has set new retail standards in book retailing and has created in, for example, stores such as Gower Street, Piccadilly (Hatchards), Birmingham, Kingston, Trafalgar Square, Newcastle, Oxford and Dublin some of the finest bookshops in the world.

All of this, of course, has cost money. The Dillons shops represent about 550,000 square foot of retail space, and the capital cost, after a modest amount of depreciation, will be around £50 million. If we assume stock at retail values of £100 per square foot (and this will now have been reduced), then the total stockholding at selling prices will be £55 million, which represents a figure of approximately £33 million at cost. As normal trade credit from suppliers will fund 70 per cent of the value of stock, this leaves 30 per cent for Dillons to finance, which amounts to £10 million. The total current investment by Pentos in the Dillons business should, therefore, be around £60 million. Dillons has been profitable in every year during this period of rapid expansion. Recent results, although still showing profits, have been clouded by a number of one-off items; however, on the basis of historic trading and stockholding policies, the underlying level of profits should be at least £7 million. This is a little less than 5 per cent of sales, but it is at the nadir of a recession (a recession in which Dillons has been mercilessly squeezed by the escalation of occupation costs) and with a high proportion of immature retail space (shops only recently opened).

The recession is now at an end; increases in rental costs have evaporated as the time lag factor has worked through the system; the new space should generate better than average sales increases as it moves closer to maturity; there remain further opportunities for improved gross margins from the better buying terms which Dillons' dominant position should now command; and the demographic factors are favourable as more people move into the age group which contains the biggest bookbuyers. The hard work has been done and the investment made; it is now a matter of fine-tuning – e.g. further systems improvement – and benefiting from the positive side of operational gearing. Dillons should, therefore, assuming the continuation of previous trading policies, now start to generate substantial improvements in profitability. And in the near future is the prospect of the abolition of the net book agreement and the significant marketing opportunities which will then be available to Dillons given its strong strategic position in the retail book market; it will be able to compete on equal terms with other retailers.

I believe that the stock market should place a high value on a retail business with these characteristics. (In the United States, book retailing is a highly regarded business sector, and all of the major book chains have identified Dillons-style superstores as the major growth opportunity.) Currently, the price earnings ratio of non-food retail companies is around 20; which means that the stock market is valuing them at twenty times their annual after-tax profits. Due to the factors I have discussed above, I believe that within a three-year period Dillons' underlying profit margin should improve from 5 per cent to 7.5 per cent; I also believe that, on very conservative estimates and without any new space, sales should increase from £150 million to £200 million; profits would therefore be £15 million. Assuming a full tax charge (despite the fact that Dillons' high recent investment programme should mean a lower tax charge for some time), and a price earnings ratio of 15 (recognising that current ratios discount an element of future profits growth), then we arrive at a valuation of £135 million for the Dillons business. Pentos's investment of £60 million does not look so bad after all.

It is also instructive to look at Smith's investment in Waterstone's. Smith's acquisition of Waterstone's in 1989 cost approaching £60 million, inclusive of bank debt and outstanding capital commitments for new shops, at a time when Waterstone's annual sales were around £40 million. Smith's then merged Waterstone's with Sherratt and Hughes, its existing specialist bookselling business. Smith's investment in Sherratt's I have assumed (I believe conservatively) to be £20 million; I have also assumed (again I think very reasonably) that a further £20 million has been invested in new shops. This would mean a total investment by Smith's in Waterstone's of £100 million compared to the Pentos investment in Dillons of £60 million; I think that Pentos has the better deal.

I believe that, on any measure, Dillons as an investment represents outstanding value; but far, far more than that has been achieved. The book trade is not the same today as it was ten years ago; Dillons bears part of the responsibility for that; we made a difference.

3

Pentos as a Retailer

It was in the second quarter of 1987 that Victor Blank suggested to me that we should consider acquiring Ryman. Ryman had had a chequered history and, over the previous twenty years, there had been several different owners, including Terence Conran and the Burton Group; it had been purchased from Burton's by a number of investors led by Jennifer d'Abo and it was now a quoted company in its own right under Jennifer's chairmanship. Ryman had, at one time, been involved in the manufacture and wholesale distribution of stationery products but it was now solely a specialist retailer of commercial and social stationery and its recent performance had improved. The idea had first been put to Victor by Jonathan Stone, a London solicitor who also liked to try his hand at deal-making. He now came to see me and explained that a number of shareholders in Ryman were dissatisfied and would not be averse to a bid. He was highly critical of Ryman's management, but I was later to discover that it was not difficult to incur Stone's displeasure and that there were few people who measured up to his exacting standards. The first thing to do, he suggested, was to meet Jennifer d'Abo to see how we got on. As it turned out, the first thing I had to do was to agree an introductory fee with Jonathan Stone, to be paid if a deal should go through, which I did without demur. It was later to turn into a bone of contention with Victor, however, as he believed that his bank, Charterhouse, was also entitled to an introductory fee and, with the strong support of the rest of the Pentos board, I had to make it clear that we could not pay two fees for the same service although we quite happily paid Charterhouse the normal merchant banking fee for handling the bid.

I met Jennifer d'Abo in her office. Jennifer is a tall, attractive, energetic woman who can be a little domineering; she has an extrovert, flamboyant personality and wears large heart-shaped spectacles; she has become something of a role model for the successful businesswoman. She explained to me early on that she could not read a balance sheet, and I was later to find out at our first board meeting that this was no exaggeration. After several meetings, and a number of false starts, the terms of a deal were agreed and were announced to the stock market in August 1987; we were to acquire Ryman on a share exchange basis which would mean the issue by Pentos of 12 million new shares which had a market value at that time of £18 million.

Ryman had a strong brand identity and would fit logically with Dillons and Athena into the specialist retail group which Pentos was creating; it had 62 shops, all of which were situated in London and the South-East of England. We saw an opportunity to create a national chain from this strong regional base; we also saw opportunities for improving focus within the shops so that the offer was clearer to customers – the original concept had become diluted and it was a matter of 'back to basics' before that became a politically embarrassing statement to make – and for revamping the dated look of the store design. Ryman was to become *the* specialist on the high street for commercial and social stationery; the offer would be range, quality, service and convenience; it would aim to supply all the needs of the small business and the ancillary and emergency requirements of the large business; the SOHO market (small office, home office) would be an important part of its target market. We recruited new senior management (Jennifer had gone off to do her own thing); Jon Isherwood introduced a down-to-earth, practical, no-nonsense shop design (this was not Athena) that was relevant to the product offer; and a move was made to a new warehouse which had the capacity to service 200 shops and which incorporated an improved, computer-based and highly efficient stock replenishment system. In 1988 we opened 12 new Ryman shops, and profits in its first full year under Pentos ownership were around £2 million, which was more than twice the level achieved in the year prior to acquisition.

Pentos's expanding retail interests had created an opportunity for property development profits. Put at its simplest, Dillons or Athena might identify a retail property from which they would wish to trade; if it were possible to purchase the freehold of the property, then, with the added value which would be created by the benefit of a lease in Athena's or Dillons' name, it could quickly be resold to an investing institution (typically a pension fund or an insurance company), at a profit. From this simplistic concept, we built a worthwhile and valuable business within Pentos. It was refined as we tackled more ambitious projects, so that we added value by the use of our property development skills as well as by the use of our retail covenants. We acquired a reputation for expertise in the refurbishment and redevelopment of buildings listed for their architectural or historical importance. This was slightly more complex: we would purchase the freehold of an old property which had the potential for conversion into prime, high-quality retail space; we would, at the same time, enter into a series of lease agreements for the completed development with retailers, which would usually include Dillons or Athena but which might also include other blue-chip high street names such as Dixons, Boots or W.H. Smith; and, also at the same time, we would enter into an agreement for the sale of the completed and fully-let development to an institution. The key point was the avoidance of risk; the proposed development had to be pre-let and pre-sold before a commitment was made to purchase; all the agreements would be entered into contemporaneously. We established a new subsidiary company named English and Overseas Properties Ltd (it had been a dormant company within English and Overseas Investments Ltd when it was acquired in 1980), to be responsible for our property development activities, and Jim Clark was appointed as its chief executive. The risk-free profits were, however, too good to last; other retailers and other property developers had their eyes on the same opportunities, and the competition for good development sites hotted up. Jim was increasingly pressing upon me the need for greater flexibility if he was to compete on equal terms; he needed to be able to move more quickly and therefore might wish to complete the purchase of a property before the final details of tenancies or sale to an institution were finalised; the risk-free nature of the transaction was being eroded. Before long, it was being suggested that we should undertake entirely speculative development projects (no pre-let and no pre-sale) which could be financed by non-recourse, off balance sheet, bank debt. I had no appetite for off balance sheet borrowings and the illusion of its non-recourse nature, and I was unhappy about the general direction of the business; the market-place had become highly competitive, and I was not prepared to take the risks which I was told would be required if Pentos was to remain a player. Fortunately, a solution which satisfied everybody was available. The Stock Exchange was going through one of its periodic bouts of overvaluing property development companies – just at a time when competitive pressures were building up and secure profits were becoming more difficult to achieve. The two simple ways of valuing companies in the stock market are either to establish the underlying net asset value, traditional for property companies, or to establish the level of sustainable earnings and apply a multiple to them – the price earnings ratio – which is the usual approach for trading companies. By the very nature of its business, the profits of a property development company cannot be said to be sustainable in the same way as, say, a retailer or a manufacturer with an established product; as each development comes to an end, a new one has to be found; there is no natural continuity. Nonetheless, in the first half of 1988, in what was to prove to be a final feeding frenzy, the stock market was valuing the small number of quoted pure property development companies at a sizeable multiple of their earnings; which meant that the market price stood at a substantial premium over the value of the underlying assets. In July 1988, we took advantage of this narrow window of opportunity and floated English and Overseas Properties plc as a separate independent company on the stock market. Jim

Clark was now able to pursue the policies which he and his board felt appropriate to its business; Pentos was free of the pressures to commit resources to what was never more than a marginal activity; and we raised £2.5 million in cash, made an extraordinary profit of £1 million, and retained a 29.9 per cent stake in the company; as we had invested none of our own funds in the business, the whole of the proceeds, including the proceeds from the eventual sale of the minority share, was profit. It was a neat outcome.

After the flotation of English and Overseas Properties, the only non-retailing activity left within Pentos was the office furniture business. Retailing sales in 1989 were £110 million and accounted for more than 75 per cent of total Pentos sales. The office furniture business had not been neglected, however, and it was now a sizeable and highly profitable company in its own right; in 1989 it made profits of £5.2 million on sales of £33 million. In the autumn of 1989 we decided to offer the business for sale; this would be the final step in the transformation of Pentos into a specialist retailer; the proceeds, which we expected to be in excess of £40 million, would help to fund our ambitious new shop opening programme. We decided to appoint a merchant bank.

Pentos had not previously had a merchant bank adviser. Charterhouse had handled the documentation of the Ryman acquisition, but this was only because of Victor's original introduction, and Charterhouse had not played any significant advisory role. For the past seventeen years, we had ourselves handled the multitude of acquisitions and disposals, and issued our own offer documents and circulars to shareholders; and this had included the famous innovative scrip issue in 1979 and the 1986 rights issue. The provision of financial advisory services had been one of the original business functions of Pentos in 1972, and a subsidiary had been established which was a licensed dealer in securities; under the regulatory regime which had existed at that time, this had enabled the subsidiary to act for the parent company in stock market matters such as issuing offer documents in take-over bids. The key players in bids and deals are the principals who handle the negotiations, the corporate lawyers who draft the documents, and the stockbrokers who place the shares; the recipe for success is to get the best possible corporate lawyer and the stockbroker with the heaviest placing power. I had never been entirely clear as to what the distinctive role of a merchant bank was other than to convene, host, and chair the interminable meetings – and to add mystique; and they get in the way of the principals. However, against my better judgement, I was persuaded, in view of the size and importance of the office furniture transaction, that we should appoint a merchant bank.

We had a beauty parade of some of the leading City merchant banks (they are not as proud as they used to be and allow themselves to be subjected to the embarrassment which this ritual can involve) and decided upon Schroders; it was appointed in November 1989 for the specific task of realising the investment in our office furniture business either by a trade sale, a flotation, or (least likely at the price we were seeking) a management buy-out. A Stock Exchange flotation was the early front-runner, and stockbrokers were provisionally appointed to handle the issue; the stock market, however, began to move against us; interest rates had hit 15 per cent, and the first swallows of recession had just been sighted; it became clear in the early part of 1990 that our plans for a flotation would have to be aborted. So that little time was lost, we had been working, in parallel, on a possible sale to a third party. Schroders had prepared an impressive sales prospectus and the outlook here seemed more encouraging; transactions were currently taking place with similar companies at the kind of price level which we were seeking. There were a number of interested parties including several from overseas. The chairman of a French company insisted on a secret meeting with me on a private airfield to which he was flying from Paris; it seemed a little cloak and dagger but we had our meeting and he seemed keen at the time, although nothing came of it. A Dutch company became interested, and there were protracted visits and negotiations, before, at the beginning of June, we reached a tentative agreement; the price was to be around £45 million. I had been invited to the opera by Win Bischoff, Schroders' chairman, with our respective wives, for Friday, June 26. It looked like being an occasion for celebration; it turned into a wake. On the Friday morning we received a telephone call to say that the deal was off; the Dutch company had apparently commissioned a report from consultants on Britain's uncertain economic prospects; the report concluded that the outlook was bleak and that Britain was headed for recession. That turned out to be the last serious opportunity for the sale of the office furniture business. The uncertainty about our economic prospects was replaced by the certainty of recession; a recession which was to last for four years. Profits from office furniture which peaked at £5.5 million in 1990 fell to £3.7 million in 1991, and, in 1992, a loss of £300,000 was incurred; trading has improved a little since then and it remains an excellent business; there is no reason why it should not again achieve substantial profits as the economy slowly recovers.

The failure to conclude the sale represented a major setback. A successful deal would have had a dramatic impact on the Pentos balance sheet and would have transformed its prospects. In addition to the cash inflow of more than £40 million, it would have realised a profit over book value of more than £25 million, as the Pentos investment in office furniture at that time was no more than £15 million. The 1989 balance sheet which had shareholders' funds of £47 million and borrowings of £13 million would, assuming net proceeds of £43 million, have been converted into shareholders' funds of £75 million and cash in the bank of £30 million. What riches; it always seemed that Pentos was under-capitalised given the scale of its ambitions, and here, at a stroke, it could have been corrected. What dreams; imagine how different would have been the events of the next three years.

The recession of 1990 to 1993 had its origins in 1988. It might well have been that world events and the normal economic cycle would have meant a recession of sorts, in any event; but, again, this recession was made deeper and longer by government economic mismanagement. This was a recession made by Nigel Lawson, extended by John Major, and concluded by Norman Lamont; and this time the hardest-hit were those who worked in offices in London and the South-East of England rather than those who worked and lived in the North. The stock markets world-wide had taken a sickening, panic-inducing, plunge on 'Black Monday' in October 1987; there was widespread speculation that a lasting stock market crash with its associated 1930s-style depression was to follow. Monetary authorities took urgent action to make this less likely; in Britain, interest rates which earlier in the year had been 11 per cent were reduced to 8½ per cent; early in 1988 they fell to 7½ per cent and, in March, Nigel Lawson, the Chancellor of the Exchequer, introduced a dramatic tax-reducing budget (the top rate of tax was reduced from 60 per cent to 40 per cent). As luck would have it, 'Black Monday' did not have the awesome consequences which had been feared, and the Chancellor's actions gave the consumer boom, which had been bubbling merrily along throughout the mid-1980s, its final kicker. It was a perfectly natural reaction to take the steps which were taken, but what was incomprehensible was the Chancellor's failure to reverse them when it became clear that a mistake had been made; his stubbornness meant that when corrective action was taken the medicine had to be all the stronger. We then had a period from 1989 to 1993 of the highest real interest rates on record, initially to damp down the economy which had been so irresponsibly over-heated, and to reduce inflation, and later to support an unsustainable currency level; John Major was being stubborn, in his turn, in seeking to stay within the exchange rate mechanism, which set an artificially high level for sterling. Of course, it all ended in tears in September 1992 when Britain was forced to make an ignominious withdrawal from the ERM and interest rates could finally be reduced, although, even then, far too slowly. We had suffered again from the twin and related evils of high real interest rates and an overvalued currency; not surprisingly the result had been the most damaging of recessions. I almost despaired of any action taken by a government which always seemed to make things worse, and to pray for a government which had minimalism as its guiding principle.

In the middle of 1990, before the full wretched nature of the recession had become clear, we were offered the opportunity of acquiring Hatchards. Hatchards was a business which I had long coveted and I had clear ideas as to how it could be improved. The recent change in ownership of its parent company had meant that it was now available, and, after some difficult negotiations, we had agreed to purchase it for £10.5 million. It was to be financed by a rights issue which would raise £22 million, the balance making a useful contribution to our burgeoning retail expansion, particularly at Dillons. Schroders were to be the underwriters and County NatWest and Carr, Kitcat and Aitken the brokers.

Kitcat and Aitken had been our stockbrokers from the start; Pentos, as a private company, had been formed in its offices. The thread of continuity through all the years had been Michael Cave, one of its former partners but now, in the jargon of modern depersonalised stockbroking, an institutional salesman. Michael was of the old school; he was no analyst, but he kept close to the companies he followed, gave an impeccable service, and was intensely loyal; and we at Pentos had also been loyal to Michael Cave. As with many traditional stockbroking houses, Kitcat and Aitken had recently had its fair share of traumas, and its then parent company, the Royal Bank of Canada, had taken a decision to close it down in about May 1990. We had been forced to appoint new brokers, and, impressed by its reputation as Britain's leading retail analyst, we had chosen County NatWest. Almost immediately, Kitcat and Aitken resurfaced in the guise of Carr, Kitcat and Aitken, with Michael Cave firmly on board; it had therefore been reappointed as our second broker, although it was clear that County NatWest was now the lead broker. The rights issue to finance the Hatchards acquisition in August 1990 was the first assignment which County NatWest was to undertake for Pentos.

Stock market conditions at that time were unsettled; interest rates were 15 per cent, the reality of recession was becoming clearer by the day, and there was an increasing awareness of the possible implications of Iraq's invasion of Kuwait. Pentos, however, again had a good story to tell, which should ensure a successful rights issue, even in a depressed market; all of our advisers were of the view that the purchase of Hatchards would be well received. So, the last thing on my mind was our ability to raise the money; the hard work had already been done; after several days of tough bargaining we had finally, in the early hours of the morning, signed an agreement to buy Hatchards, subject only to the rights issue; all we had to do now was to press the button. I had not been in my office many minutes, after the all-night session of final negotiations, when I received a telephone call from Nigel Saxby-Soffe, the Schroders director who handled our affairs. He told me that County NatWest had just informed him that they could not organise the sub-underwriting of the rights issue as, in the present mood of the stock market, there was no appetite for issues of this nature. I was shocked and bewildered by his news. There had been no change in stock market sentiment in the several weeks which had passed since the exercise was started; and there had been no hint, prior to this, that there might be a problem. Although a merchant bank takes the overall responsibility for underwriting a share issue, it relies on the stockbroker to arrange the sub-underwriting with institutions; and if the broker says that this cannot be done then there is no issue. I asked Nigel Saxby-Soffe to arrange an immediate meeting with the brokers so that we could discuss the matter; this he agreed to do, although he was not optimistic about the outcome. 'They have not reached this decision lightly,' he said, 'and they are hardly likely to change their minds now.'

We met at eleven o'clock in a Schroders boardroom; Nigel, in the time-honoured manner, took the chair; representatives from County NatWest and from Carr, Kitcat and Aitken gathered round the table, and I sat next to Michael Cave. Michael had expressed his dismay to me before entering the room, and had said that, if County NatWest could not deliver, then he thought that Kitcat could do it alone; I was encouraged by this support, but knew that Schroders would now require more comfort than that; they had clearly been shaken by what they had heard. Nigel asked County NatWest if they would explain the situation as they now saw it. They responded by repeating, without elaboration, the same bald message which Nigel had already conveyed to me on the telephone. I expressed my incomprehension, and pressed them to say what had changed since they had agreed to handle the issue. I received no satisfactory answer: they simply repeated, parrot fashion, that there was no sub-underwriting market; it had completely dried up. I could see that we were not going to make any progress with County NatWest, and I turned to Michael Cave and suggested to him that he telephoned, here and now, from the meeting, the two largest shareholders in Pentos, to tell them about the acquisition of Hatchards and the proposed rights issue and to get their reaction. It was a high-risk strategy, because, if they turned it down, in the hearing of all those present in the room, then that would be the end; however, I could not see that we had anything to lose as County NatWest were certainly not going to perform, and Nigel had already made it clear that without them Schroders could not underwrite the issue. Nigel confirmed that the approach which I had now suggested would not break any Stock Exchange rules, so long as it was made clear at the outset that those telephoned had become 'insiders'; Michael then undertook to make the calls. His first call was to Nicola Horlick, a fund manager at Mercury Asset Management (MAM), who at that time held around 15 per cent of the issued share capital of Pentos. He explained to her straightaway that what he was about to tell her would make her an insider, and, after she had confirmed that she was willing to accept the restrictions which that would impose, he revealed that he was speaking from Schroders, in my presence and that of others, and he outlined our plans. He said that he was taking the unusual step of calling her in this way because of the difficult stock market conditions, and he asked whether MAM, in the circumstances outlined, could give an indication of the proportion of new shares it would be prepared to underwrite. After only a moment's hesitation, Nicola Horlick said that she fully supported the proposal to purchase Hatchards and to raise further funds to take advantage of the particular opportunities for retail expansion which existed in the present environment; she said that Mercury would be prepared to underwrite 20 per cent of the issue. His next call was to Flemings who spoke for a little less than 10 per cent of the Pentos shares. He asked to speak to John Redwood, the fund manager responsible for the Pentos shareholding, and was told he was not at his desk. This threw us slightly, as time was short, and I suggested that Michael should speak to John Manser who was the chairman of Flemings and would not normally be involved in matters such as this; but we had both known him well for many years and it was worth a try. John came to the telephone straightaway, was told the story, and, in his usual laconic manner, said that Redwood was probably in the gym (Flemings has a sports club in the basement of its building) but that we could put Flemings down for 15 per cent. When Michael was off the telephone, Nigel chipped in to say that Schroders' funds would, on their own account, underwrite 10 per cent. In half an hour, 45 per cent of the issue had been underwritten. I said quietly to the County NatWest executives, who had been looking increasingly uncomfortable, that we had underwritten almost one half of the shares and could they underwrite the other half; they said that they could. The meeting, which had lasted little more than an hour, was then concluded, and the County NatWest representatives filed sheepishly from the room. In a single day, I had seen the best and the worst of the City; and I had witnessed an impressive example of the awesome power of the institutions. The rights issue was launched the following day, on August 16. Michael Cave told me that it was taken up by every fund manager to whom it was put – which was almost unprecedented; it had been an unqualified success.

There was to be a sequel. In June the following year, Pentos placed a small number of shares with institutions, as allowed under stock market regulations, to finance the purchase of some retail properties. Perhaps not surprisingly, in view of our previous experience, we asked Carr, Kitcat and Aitken to transact the business. County NatWest, as the principal Pentos broker, would normally have expected to be involved. I should, as a matter of courtesy, have informed them, but it was a minor transaction, and it never occurred to me. They were livid. Two days later, we were abruptly informed that County NatWest had resigned as stockbroker to Pentos; we had made a powerful enemy.

4

The Campaign Against the Net Book Agreement

In the early part of 1988 I was asked by the Booksellers' Association to address its annual conference, which was being held in May of that year at Bournemouth. Dillons is a member of the Booksellers' Association, despite the fact that we have little in common. The Booksellers' Association is a weak, protectionist, conservative organisation which is very much the poor relation (in terms of power and influence if not in money) of the Publishers' Association. W.H. Smith, its dominant member, use it when it suits them, but, as their ample weight would allow, ignore it when it doesn't. The publishers have run rings around the booksellers. The change in the rules and regulations of book clubs and the extension of direct sales to libraries, universities and other institutions are recent examples of moves which have been against the interests of bookshops but in which the Booksellers' Association has been powerless; ironically it is the restrictive nature of the net book agreement (NBA) which gives the publishers their power and which creates these anomalies. Dillons belongs to the Booksellers' Association for one reason: without membership it is not possible to sell or exchange book tokens; and book tokens are a very important source of business for bookshops. The company Book Tokens Ltd is a wholly owned subsidiary of the Booksellers' Association and dealing in book tokens is confined entirely to members of the Association. (Perhaps this is another restrictive practice within the book trade which should be examined by Sir Bryan Carsberg at the Office of Fair Trading?) In addition to these monopolistic powers, ensuring a healthy membership of the Booksellers' Association, it also ensures a healthy bank balance as Book Tokens Ltd is highly profitable; so, in contrast to the Publishers' Association, which never has any money, the Booksellers' Association is relatively rich.

At the Bournemouth conference I delivered a wide-ranging speech covering many aspects of the book trade and made a number of predictions for the end of the century, many of which have already come true. The main thrust of the speech (it was titled 'The Impact of Change') was on marketing and distribution: widening the market for books. Inevitably, in this context, I spoke of the restrictions imposed by the NBA (which prevents a bookseller from selling a book at less than its cover price) and its abolition was listed as one of my predictions; but it accounted for only a minor part of the speech. Nevertheless, such are the passions aroused within the book trade by the subject that for the remainder of the conference delegates talked of little else. The following day it was picked up by the newspapers; a bookseller arguing for the abolition of price control on books – it seemed to them rather like turkeys voting for Christmas. There was a follow-up story in the Sunday papers; and they had been successful in obtaining a highly provocative quote from Clive Bradley of the Publishers' Association (our first public joust) in which he promised legal action if Dillons were to break the NBA – which was a little premature given that we had at that time threatened no such thing; it was an early example of his tendency to get his retaliation in first. However, the media loved the apparent confrontation and the whiff of the courts; and from this unplanned beginning was born Dillons' campaign for the abolition of the NBA.

The campaign developed a momentum of its own; but its timing suited Dillons' overall strategy as the growing national chain would soon justify a national marketing programme and this would be seriously inhibited by the existence of the NBA. The media interest was sustained throughout the remaining months of 1988. Most journalists, in common with their readers, had not realised that book prices were controlled. Calls to me would often start with the question: 'What is the net book agreement?' But journalists read and buy books; and many of them write them. They often knew from personal experience of the inefficiencies of the book trade and they had a vested interest in keeping the debate alive.

In September 1988 I visited Blackpool where the Social and Liberal Democrats (as I think they were then momentarily called) were having their annual conference. I was still a committed and enthusiastic Liberal and I was to have dinner with Paddy Ashdown. The morning following the dinner, as I was checking out of the hotel, I saw Richard Holme (now Lord Holme of Cheltenham). I had known Richard for many years although not well. We were both long-standing Liberals, but Richard, as a close adviser and speech writer to both David Steel and Paddy Ashdown, was far more prominent and active than I. Richard came over to me and after the usual preliminaries he asked what was happening on the NBA. I told him that I believed that Dillons was now strong enough to mount an offensive and that 1989 could be the 'crunch' year. So far we had merely been debating but soon it would be the time for action. Richard said that he thought he could help; with Dick Taverne and Roger Liddle he had recently established a consultancy specialising in what he described as 'issue management'. We agreed to meet and Richard and Roger came to my offices for our first meeting on October 7. They were both to become key members of our team and highly stimulating colleagues and friends. (Richard Holme and Roger Liddle, together with my colleagues Frank Brazier and Julian Rivers and my secretary Jill Copping, who claimed with justification to have the best list of media contacts in London, were, with myself, the team which 'ran' the NBA campaign. In the narrative which follows I have often, for reasons of economy, used the term 'we' as shorthand for the core group.)

We soon agreed a timetable of events and a list of specific tasks. A document was to be prepared which would set out our case in a formal and academic manner; we would establish a list of communication targets amongst the media, 'opinion formers', and 'the great and the good', in an attempt to seize what we described as the moral and intellectual high ground; together with our lawyers we would prepare a formal complaint to lodge with the Office of Fair Trading to seek a review and subsequent reference to the Restrictive Practices Court; and most importantly we would seek to co-ordinate support from those publishers who shared our opposition to the NBA and who might be persuaded to leave it unilaterally. We had fixed on a date towards the end of March as a tentative 'D' day when we would make a public statement of our intentions; we would hope by that time to have some positive publisher reaction. This timetable was, however, blown dramatically off course by the sheer pressure of media interest.

Journalists writing their New Year stories were constantly telephoning me to ask when they could expect action on the NBA. This was a story they really did want to write about; they needed no encouragement from me. We decided to ride with the flood of the tide. I gave an interview to Martin Bailey of the *Observer*, a journalist who had been particularly persistent, and on January 8, 1989 a front-page story in the *Observer* was headlined: 'Bookshops set for cut price war'. It quoted me as saying that during the course of the year Dillons would make a definite move to reduce the price of certain key titles. It was a modest statement but it offered the promise of action rather than words, which the media had been hoping for; and there was the by now normal over-reaction and threat of writs from the Publishers' Association which helped to make the story. The *Sunday Times* picked up the *Observer* story for its later editions; the following day it was featured in all the nationals and was on the radio news bulletins. We decided that now was the time to pile in and to hell with the timetable. As the American Admiral Stephen Decatur said in the War of 1812, 'Damn the torpedoes! Full speed ahead!' Roger and Richard lobbied hard with their editorial contacts in Fleet Street. On January 10 there was a leader in *The Times*; on the 11th there were leaders in the *Independent* and the *Guardian*; the tabloids followed suit; on January 14 it was the turn of the *Economist*; all were favourable. *The Times* agreed to publish a 1,500-word article by me on the op-ed page in its Saturday edition on January 14. In this I wrote of the 'deadly mixture of élitism and pessimism which seems to characterise those publishers still resisting reform: élitism in believing that books are only for "people like us" who know what they want and where to find it; and a pessimism which assumes that the demand for books is finite and that what is put in one pocket must be taken from another'. I took off for my regular January skiing holiday in St Moritz but was pursued on the slopes by the *Today* programme. This was now a fully fledged, fully paid-up campaign; and we had made a major step towards our objective of capturing the intellectual high ground. But what was now absolutely critical was the need to get friendly publishers on our side; we had made a promise and we had to deliver.

In the midst of this frenzy of activity there was an amusing interlude. In the final weeks of 1988 I had a telephone enquiry and then a letter from a Pamella Bordes at the House of Commons. She was working with David Shaw MP, who was later to attempt unsuccessfully to introduce a private member's bill to abolish the NBA, and she was seeking my views. This was followed by a meeting in my office attended by both David Shaw and Miss Bordes. She arrived after Shaw and sat looking nondescript and slightly sorry for herself in a long raincoat, uttering hardly a word. The three of us left my office together and I escorted them into the street and towards my car, which I had offered for their return to the House of Commons. David Shaw wished to collect a package from a nearby shop and so I was left alone for two or three minutes with Miss Bordes. 'What did you do before you worked in the House of Commons?' I asked of her, not very originally. 'I was a beauty queen,' she replied. I am not often at a loss for words, but on this occasion I did struggle to find anything else to say. Shortly afterwards, there was a newspaper photograph of an extremely glamorous girl in a car with the then Minister for Sport, Colin Moynihan; she was named as Pamella Bordes. When she later called me to check some material I mentioned that she had looked quite different in the photograph. 'Ah,' she said, 'I had a cold when I came to see you.' The debate over the NBA has certainly attracted participants from all walks of life.

1989, the first full year of the campaign, was dominated by two issues: the need to persuade a sufficient number of publishers to publish titles non-net (or to agree to take no action should Dillons discount net titles) so that we could redeem our pledge to discount certain key titles during the course of the year; and the need to convince Sir Gordon Borrie, the Director General of the Office of Fair Trading, that he should refer the NBA to the Restrictive Practices Court. We were to fail on both counts; although the outside world would not fully realise this, as we continued to build on our success in increasing public awareness both of Dillons and of the evils of the NBA; and we did, in fact, launch, towards the end of the year, a promotion of sorts which featured new titles at discounted prices.

I have always believed that the most likely way in which the NBA would be made ineffective would be by the unilateral action of individual publishers leaving the agreement; and that it would then wither on the vine. Some publishers had already made clear their opposition to the agreement (Faber, Bloomsbury, Octopus, and less consistently Century Hutchinson); some were 'fight to the last ditch' supporters (Penguin, Hodder, Transworld); but most, despite the protestations of the Publishers' Association, were uncertain. It was our task to win over some of the waverers and to convince our supporters that they should act now on their conviction either by leaving the agreement altogether or by publishing certain titles non-net on an experimental basis. In any event, we would argue, the agreement's days were numbered because of impending action either by the Office of Fair Trading, or Parliament, or the European Commission, and because of the sheer weight of public opinion; so why wait, why not act now? We would also demonstrate that they would sell more books as a result of more aggressive, sophisticated and focused marketing; so that it was very much in their commercial interest.

The targeted publishers were divided primarily between myself and Frank Brazier and we started the long process of individual meetings and lunches. It was soon clear that the smaller, supportive publishers were not prepared to take any initiatives on their own, but would need the comfort of the involvement of at least one of the larger publishers; and the hidden hand of W.H. Smith was a constant presence at our discussions. The attitude of Octopus, the one large trade publisher which was unequivocal in its support of our stand, was clearly going to be crucial.

The Octopus Publishing Group was founded by Paul Hamlyn in 1971. It acquired Heinemann in 1985, and it was in turn acquired by Reed International in 1987. Paul remained chairman of Octopus, a director of Reed, and was Reed's largest shareholder. Paul had been good for the book trade and the book trade had been very good to Paul. Few people have made a greater contribution to its development in the past forty years and nobody – absolutely nobody – has made anything like as much money as Paul from his involvement. He is a marketing genius and a passionate free marketeer. He has always been opposed to the NBA. Ironically, his first publishing company, the Paul Hamlyn Group, was acquired by the precursor of Reed, International Publishing Corporation (when he made his first fortune) in 1964. He left in 1970 following the merger between Reed and IPC; which was when I first met him. He was then, in 1970, unbelievably, joint managing director of the *News of the World*. The other joint managing director was Rupert Murdoch. The idea of either of these powerful, individualistic tycoons sharing power with any other person was bizarre and yet here they were sharing it with each other. It was a temporary resting place. At one of our early meetings Paul mentioned to me his plans to start a new publishing venture; he never wanted a large organisation again, he told me. This new company (Octopus) would employ only a few creative people; he would publish books for a single customer and would not have worries about distribution and sales ledgers and debt collection and all the other problems of administration. In fact, Octopus has developed into one of Britain's largest publishing houses and has achieved enormous success. Although I have known Paul Hamlyn for many years and value our friendship, I do not know him well. Few people do. He is intensely private and has an unnerving habit of introducing long pauses into conversations which his companion feels the need to fill. I am sure that it is a very good negotiating tactic.

Ian Irvine, a former partner of the accountants Touche Ross, had been appointed chief executive of Octopus prior to its acquisition by Reed, and Paul had handed over the day-to-day executive responsibilities to him. So it was with Ian that I had the first discussion with regard to our plans for breaking the NBA. We had lunch together on February 17, 1989. It went well and it was left that Frank Brazier would be in touch with Richard Charkin, who then had responsibility for the particular publishing imprints which were involved, to agree the specific titles which we would wish to include in the promotion, the launch of which was now planned for May. Things went less well thereafter. Problems started to arise on details such as discounts and quantities; and then when we conceded on these we were told of concerns about the wider economic and commercial considerations – code for W.H. Smith. The negotiations culminated in a letter to me from Ian Irvine dated March 28 in which he concluded, 'In summary, we will of course supply your order at your normal terms but I must let you know that we feel bound to support the Publishers' Association in whatever action they take should you discount these titles.' It would be difficult to be more uncompromising than that; and it represented a complete volte face from our discussions over lunch on February 17; but Reed had extensive magazine interests in addition to books – and Smith's hidden hand had clearly shed its velvet glove. I had to speak to Paul. I caught him in his office and he said that he knew there had been difficulties but that he would speak to Ian to get fully up to date and he would then call me at home at the weekend. (One of the many coincidences in this small world is that our house in the country is the former home of Paul and his wife Helen.) He rang me on the Sunday morning and said straightaway, 'Terry, I cannot help you.' He said he was very sorry, but that there were wider implications at Reed and that I could not rely on Octopus for support. I was very distressed and felt let down (as we shall see, Reed were to be far bolder and braver in 1991); Octopus were central to our planned initiative; without Octopus there was no promotion. We immediately aborted our plans for a May launch. Fortunately, we had been careful in our public comments and our only stated commitment was for a price-led promotion before the year's end; we still had time; but we had been very badly shaken. We had also been fortunate with the distraction which had been provided by the developments with the Office of Fair Trading. So we decided to see how the OFT issue was to be resolved before making any further plans.

Dillons had sent a closely argued submission to the Director General of Fair Trading on February 14, setting out the reasons why we believed he should apply to the courts for a review of the 1962 decision to uphold the NBA. On April 28, Sir Gordon Borrie announced that he had ordered a 'wide enquiry into the current effects of the net book agreement'; a prerequisite of any formal application to the courts. This was a minor but important victory for Dillons. Officials at the Office of Fair Trading would now collect evidence from all interested parties and a final decision was promised for the end of July. The legal hurdles which had to be overcome, however, were tough; Sir Gordon would not be making a judgement on whether the NBA was a good or a bad thing; he would simply be deciding whether there had been a sufficient materiality of change since 1962 for the courts to arrive at a different conclusion. So much had changed in the world in the intervening twenty-five years, not least as a result of the Resale Prices Act of 1964, that this might not have seemed a difficult task. Dillons' lawyers, however, had always stressed the stringent legal tests which have to be satisfied for re-opening a judgement which the Restrictive Practices Court has already made.

Dillons' fourteen pages of evidence catalogued the major changes (without necessarily signifying either approval or disapproval) which had taken place in the book trade since 1962: the transformation of a cottage publishing industry into one dominated by conglomerates and multi-nationals; the development of robust retail chains; the growth of book clubs and W.H. Smith's own-brand books, both of which were permitted under the net book agreement but which represented a distortion of free retail competition; and new technology which had made entry into the publishing industry cheaper and easier. We pointed to experience in other countries where book prices were lower and book sales were higher; Britain was the only English-language country which still had price control on books. The French experience was often quoted gleefully by our opponents. In France, their version of the NBA had been abolished in 1979 but then hurriedly re-introduced in 1981 as a result of panic and confusion in the book trade. The mistake the French made, I patiently explained, was to abolish the cover price of the book; which nobody in their right mind was advocating for this country, and indeed in every other country which operates a free market the recommended retail price continues to be shown boldly on the jacket. The main debate, however, revolved around the growth in book prices. Our evidence showed that book prices had increased at twice the rate of inflation for most of the 1980s. Dr Fishwick, employed by the Publishers' Association to submit evidence on its behalf to the Office of Fair Trading, produced figures which, from its standpoint, were more reassuring. The statisticians got involved. If ever there was a case to show that figures could be used to prove almost anything this seemed to be it. Separate indices were prepared according to the different doctrines of Laspeynes, Paasche, Fisher and Tourquist – names apparently as familiar to statisticians as Freud and Jung are to psychoanalysts. A seventeen-page supplementary document was prepared; we settled on a 'chained book Laspeynes' index which was on the same basis as the retail price index – and which showed that book prices had risen substantially more than the RPI. It was impossible for its defenders to continue their surprising claim, which in any event was contrary to the normal expectations of economic theory, that the NBA kept book prices down.

On the afternoon of August 2 I received a telephone call from an official at the Office of Fair Trading. He told me that he was about to fax me a copy of a press release which was to be issued the following morning; he warned me that I might not be happy with its contents. I stood by the fax machine as the announcement came through; 'Sir Gordon Borrie, Director General of Fair Trading, today announced that he will not seek leave of the Restrictive Practices Court to have the net book agreement reconsidered.' He gave two reasons: he conceded that there had been many changes in the book trade since 1962 but, he said, 'I have had to consider whether these changes are of such magnitude as to lead to a different conclusion . . . I have concluded that there is an insufficiently strong basis to justify me in making an application to the Court to reopen the case'; and he added, 'I have also had regard to the fact that the Government has proposed new legislation which would require me to review all agreements with restrictions previously upheld by the Restrictive Practices Court.'

I was bitterly disappointed; we had been encouraged by our recent discussions with Sir Gordon's officials and felt that there had been a last-minute change of mind; the Government statement on competition policy, rather than being helpful, had actually allowed Sir Gordon to continue to sit on the fence; which was becoming an occupational hazard for those involved in this lengthening dispute. I immediately rushed out a press release accusing Sir Gordon of timidity; said that he had given too great a weight to special pleading from the more conservative elements in the book trade and not enough to the interests of the consumer; and called on the Government to introduce its promised legislation on competition policy without delay. It concluded: 'The fight to end the net book agreement goes on.'

The media round began again. I was on breakfast news and then on television and radio news bulletins throughout the day; each time the Dillons position (and often a shot of a Dillons bookshop) was the lead on the story; and the press accepted totally that this was no more than a stay of execution; we had certainly made the best of a major setback.

Throughout the campaign, I had kept key politicians informed of our views and actions and this had included the Prime Minister and the different Ministers who from time to time had responsibility for competition policy. On March 13 I received a letter from Francis Maude who was at that time Parliamentary Under-Secretary of State for Corporate Affairs. It was a supportive letter. He said that 'my department will be watching with close interest the outcome of your submission to the Office of Fair Trading' and 'in the meantime, you may be interested to note that the Government is developing proposals for fundamental changes to existing restrictive trade practices legislation'. He went on to say that 'the net book agreement would then need to be considered afresh under the new criteria in due course'. In July, the Government duly published its White Paper on 'Opening Markets: New Policy on Restrictive Practices'; it was this document to which Sir Gordon Borrie had referred when deciding not to send the NBA back to the courts. Under these new proposals, the test would not be whether it was possible to reopen a decision a court has already made but whether the NBA satisfied new criteria where the presumption is against restrictive agreements of any kind.

Five years later we are still waiting for the promised legislation. This was to the obvious embarrassment of Francis Maude's successor, John Redwood, who in several meetings and also in letters to me confirmed the Government's intentions but in postscripts would add 'this requires agreement about priorities in a packed programme'. The Government's inaction has been in stark contrast to Ted Heath's stubborn, determined and brave single-mindedness in 1964; it enabled Sir Gordon Borrie to procrastinate until the end of his time in office; and the absence of any firm proposals in the Queen's speech in October 1993 has now led Sir Gordon's successor, Sir Bryan Carsberg, to order (in frustration, as his statement makes clear) a further, wide-ranging enquiry – which we will come to in due course. In the meantime, the consumer has suffered book prices higher than ever and the book trade has been damaged by continuing uncertainty.

In November 1989 Dillons launched what we described as a 'Christmas experiment in promoted price reduction'. We had spent the first half of the year in trying, unsuccessfully, to persuade publishers to publish new mainstream titles outside the net book agreement. Defenders of the status quo often argued that publishers had the flexibility within the agreement to publish non-net if they so wished and that, therefore, it was not quite the ogre which its attackers portrayed. The fact was that this flexibility had not been used and we had seen at first hand the pressures brought to bear, should it be contemplated, by those who wished to restrict competition. However, there was one exception. The early Octopus imprints had been published non-net in accordance with Paul Hamlyn's principles and beliefs. The titles concerned were non-fiction and not obviously part of mainstream publishing; we had seen that even Paul Hamlyn had been unable to prevail so far as the new imprints which he had developed or acquired, and which included a wide range of quality fiction, were concerned. The non-net titles included a number (e.g. Hugh Johnson's *Pocket Wine Book* and *Millers Antique Price Guide*) which were particularly attractive at Christmas time for gifts; and despite the fact that they were non-net they had always been treated by the trade as net books and had never been sold, whilst new books, below their cover price. So this was an opportunity to honour our promise to discount certain new titles by the end of the year and to obtain evidence to support our belief that promoted price reductions would bring more people into bookshops and would sell more books. These were not the high-profile quality fiction titles with which ideally we wished to associate Dillons and it was not the major broadside against the NBA for which we had hoped, but it was the best we could do. The promotion was announced at a press conference on November 16; the prices of eight selected titles were reduced by between 20 per cent and 25 per cent backed by a £250,000 advertising campaign. Journalists were initially a little sceptical (not unusual) as they saw that the titles were non-net and therefore this was not the breach of the NBA which they had been more than half-expecting. However, they recognised that we were breaking new ground – it had never been done before – and that it would inevitably place the agreement under further pressure. There was another media blitz with Dillons bookstores featured prominently on all television news stories and Dillons' name mentioned repeatedly in radio news bulletins. The newspaper coverage again included an editorial in *The Times*. It described the promotion as 'a shot from a pop-gun rather than a heavy artillery salvo', but it went on: 'It does not look as if Mr Maher is going to go away. There are shrewd men in publishing, too, and many of them realise that the broader Maher manifesto is not without its attraction. If he succeeds in widening the market for books, that will be in their interest' – and it *was* a *Times* leader. A December article in *Publishing News* commented: 'Can there be any amongst us, even the strongest NBA supporter, who does not have a sneaking admiration for the way the battle has been led? The new promotion emphatically breaks new ground. The campaign itself has so far been run all but faultlessly.' Little did they know. However, the fact remained that the year had ended better than had, on more than one occasion, seemed likely.

1990 started with the announcement of the results of the promotion and was to end with the high drama of the Booker discount offer. In February, I wrote to all the leading publishers with the key facts from the Christmas experiment in promoted price reduction: sales of the promoted titles had increased fivefold and 50 per cent of discount book purchasers also bought at least two other books (a figure which was to recur with uncanny consistency in all the subsequent promotions and which made the critical point about the importance of secondary purchases). I called upon publishers to review their planned titles (of quality fiction) for the autumn and to indicate openly which they were prepared to declare non-net in order to facilitate selective price promotion – not just by Dillons but by any bookseller. Approached in this way, I argued (I thought reasonably), the book trade as a whole could loosen the constraints which are holding back further development: a plea which was to fall largely on deaf ears.

Gordon Graham is one of the more thoughtful members of the book trade. He was chairman of Butterworth's from 1975 to 1990 and a former president of the Publishers' Association; since he retired from Butterworth's he has founded and is editor of *Logos*, which he describes as the professional journal for the book world. He is a widely-travelled Scotsman who has acquired US nationality. We have much in common, not least a passionate love for skiing in the Engadine. He was concerned about the emotion which had been raised over the NBA issue and wondered whether there was not a middle way forward. I arranged a lunch in my office for May 31 and invited Gordon and Anthony Cheetham, now chairman of the newly-merged Random Century; Richard Holme and my colleagues Frank Brazier and Julian Rivers were also there, and Terry Kitson, who was at the beginning of his short reign as chief executive of Collins, could not make the lunch but joined us for coffee. There was a broad measure of agreement that a way must be found through the impasse. Gordon said that he planned to write an article which he hoped the *Bookseller* would publish and which he believed could move the debate forward in a constructive manner. The article, titled 'A bridgeable gap?', appeared on July 13. He advocated a third category of books, in addition to net and non-net, which he suggested should be called RRP. He made the legitimate point that, when the NBA had been drawn up in 1890, the category non-net had been designed primarily for text books sold in bulk to the educational market and not for titles for the general trade; and this, he argued, could be a reason for resistance to the idea of publishing general trade titles as non-net. His proposed new category RRP (recommended retail price) could, he suggested, be used for hardcover titles of quality fiction and hoped-for bestsellers, selected by their publishers, to be sold individually to the public in bookshops at prices determined by the booksellers. I immediately issued a statement of support for what I described as a major new initiative (a kiss of death, some might think). I said that his proposals for reform clearly fell short of Dillons' objective (which continued to be the abolition of the NBA) but said that, if they were shown to command consensus within the trade, before the promised full regulatory review by the competition authorities, then Dillons would offer its full co-operation. I believed, in any event, that, as publishers experienced the benefits of greater flexibility, the NBA would soon be left behind them. From the rest of the trade there was a deathly silence.

It was the sense of frustration arising from our failure to persuade any publisher to take any initiative at all, despite their stated wish for change, added to the increased strength which Dillons felt as the result of the acquisition of Hatchards (it had been purchased by Dillons in August), which led to the decision, taken in September, to discount unilaterally the Booker shortlisted titles.

The Booker Prize is the most prestigious literary prize in Britain. It is presented to the author of what is judged to be the best new work of fiction published each year and he or she receives a cheque for £25,000. The shortlist had recently been published and the winner was to be announced at a dinner at the Guildhall on Tuesday, October 16.

The shortlist consisted of six titles. Five were from publishing houses which were either outright opponents of the NBA or favoured substantial reform. They were amongst the publishers with whom I had been discussing de-netting. As a number of publishers would be involved, it would not be possible for Smith's to pick off individual publishers and, since Dillons had not selected the shortlist, Smith's could not suggest collusion with the publishers concerned. We were proposing to reduce the price of the Booker shortlisted titles although all were published as net books under the NBA. Clearly, therefore, we would be breaking the NBA. The 1962 ruling of the Restrictive Practices Court meant in effect that despite the 1964 Resale Prices Act the NBA under UK law was a lawful agreement. However, the European Commission had on December 12, 1989 made a decision with wide implications. It had ruled that the NBA was in breach of the Treaty of Rome. The Publishers' Association had appealed to the European Court and had sought to play down the significance of the decision. The legal issues were complicated but, nonetheless, the advice which we had received from our lawyers was clear and unequivocal: the NBA had lost its provisional validity from which it had benefited since the accession of the United Kingdom to the EEC in 1973 and the Commission's decision meant that, despite the outstanding appeal (which has since been dismissed although a further final appeal has been made), the NBA is void and ceases to be enforceable in the UK. Therefore, if we were to proceed to discount the Booker shortlist, we would not be breaking the law. This was crucial. However, our lawyer inevitably cautioned us that, if the Publishers' Association were to apply to the courts for an injunction, then there was at least a 50 per cent chance that they would be successful as the courts might prove reluctant to involve themselves in the European aspects until a full hearing. That advice was to prove prophetic.

We decided to go ahead and sell the six titles on the Booker shortlist at least 25 per cent below their published price. We calculated that if the promotion was announced on a Friday morning then even if the Publishers' Association were successful in obtaining an injunction it would not be until after the weekend. That would mean at worst the benefits of a buoyant weekend's takings, a major public relations coup, and the possibility of a fatal blow to the NBA. Much would depend on the response and the resolve of the publishers – our fragile Achilles heel. We fixed October 12 as the day on which we would make our move. On October 1 we ordered substantial quantities of each of the titles from the respective publishers so that we would be well stocked and not at risk from a suspension of supply. As the orders were around four times the normal order quantity it was inconceivable that the publishers concerned did not realise that something unusual was happening and this meant that there was a serious risk of a breach of security. However, we had no alternative, and although there were rumblings in the trade our luck held.

I arrived at my office in New Bond Street early on Friday, October 12. A press conference had been called for eleven o'clock. Point-of-sale material was waiting to be unveiled in over one hundred bookshops throughout the country and advertising space had been reserved in the weekend papers.

As I sat at my desk I reviewed the long list of telephone calls I wanted to make before the press conference. The first calls were courtesy calls to Booker and to the five publishing houses to inform them of our plans ahead of the formal announcement. I called Jonathan Taylor at Booker; he was then its chief executive but is now its chairman. I knew Jonathan reasonably well through my membership of the committee of the Bodleian Library campaign of which he was chairman. He too opposed the NBA, as did Booker's chairman Sir Michael Caine, so I did not expect any real problems, although I was anxious that he should not think that we were seeking to upstage Booker in any way. His response was immediate and enthusiastic: the publicity would help the Booker Prize and give it a higher profile; he supported totally any move to kill the NBA; and he offered his congratulations for an imaginative marketing coup.

I next spoke to Nigel Newton who is the chairman and founder of Bloomsbury, the publisher of *Lies of Silence* by Brian Moore. It was fairly widely known at that time that Nigel was against the NBA. He had made his views clear to me in conversation and he had expressed them equally clearly at a recent meeting of the Royal Society of Arts at which he had presented a paper – the meeting had been chaired by Sir Simon Hornby, the chairman of W.H. Smith, who had responded in a vigorous and ill-tempered manner to Nigel's unwelcome remarks. We had a brief but friendly chat. I put it very specifically to him that I assumed he would not be taking any action to frustrate our plans. He replied, 'Terry, you know me, I might huff and puff in public but judge me by my actions not my words.' I suppose, looking literally at the phraseology he used, that it could mean anything; but I had no doubt from our conversation what he meant me to understand.

I then rang Anthony Cheetham who was the chief executive of Random Century (now Random House), owners of Chatto and Windus, the publisher of two of the shortlisted titles, *Solomon Gorsky Was Here* by

Mordecai Richler and *Possession* (the eventual winner) by A.S. Byatt. Anthony was a leading advocate of, at the very least, a major reform of the NBA. He had taken part in the meetings in my office at which we had discussed how we could move to de-netting certain general trade titles – just the kind of important literary titles which were on the Booker shortlist. Sadly, my experiences with Anthony are that he promises rather more than he delivers. However, in our telephone conversation he was generally supportive and I did not anticipate any problems from Chatto.

The next call was to Matthew Evans, the chairman of Faber and Faber, the publisher of *Amongst Women* by John McGahern. Matthew likes to see himself as a bit of a maverick within the book trade. On the NBA he was unequivocal in his outright opposition; and this had called for some courage when his most important and famous author, William Golding, took him to task on the matter. However, in my dealings with Matthew, I was never quite sure that I was being told the whole story. On this occasion, he appeared disarmingly frank; 'so far as the outside world is concerned,' he said, 'I will be in Ireland for the next week. I plan to do nothing.' This was Matthew's equivalent of a diplomatic illness. He was going to keep well out of the way.

The publisher of *The Gate of Angels* by Penelope Fitzgerald, the fifth shortlisted Booker title, was Collins. Collins had been in a state of some managerial turmoil since its acquisition by Rupert Murdoch's interests in 1989. After the take-over, Ian Chapman, Collins' long-standing and highly-respected chairman and chief executive, had left, and the subsequent management appointments had not been a success. As a result, Terry Kitson, who had made his reputation as head of Collins in Australia, had recently been appointed chief executive and he was dividing his time between Australia and Britain. Terry's heart did not seem to be engaged in the appointment, however, and it seemed to me very much a stop-gap arrangement; Terry was looking forward to his retirement in his adopted Australia. In my talks with him about the NBA he had been cautious but precise. There was no price control in Australia and he did not believe there should be price control in the UK. As a first move, he favoured selective de-netting. When asked if Collins would support legal action against Dillons should we take an initiative in breaching the NBA, he said that they would not but that they would wish to discuss the matter with us. I called Terry Kitson's office in London; and I was told that he was in Australia. I then spoke to his newly appointed deputy, Eddie Bell, whom I barely knew. Eddie is a jovial, extrovert salesman; he is a little larger than life in more ways than one. He can give the appearance of being a buffoon but his rapid progress since joining Collins from Hodder and Stoughton is proof that appearances can be deceptive. Eddie was his usual friendly and cheerful self on the telephone and seemed vastly amused by my news. He gave no indication that he had any objection to our action.

My final call to a publisher was to Colin Haycraft, the chairman of Duckworth, the publisher of *An Awfully Big Adventure* by Beryl Bainbridge. Although I did not then know Colin and did not know his stance on the NBA, I was aware of his reputation as a man of strongly held independent views. In our brief conversation he was friendly and seemed to be looking forward to the increased book sales which were now in contemplation.

Just before the press conference I had a brief meeting with Frank and Julian. The response from publishers had been better than expected. So long as they held firm we would be home and dry.

The press conference was crowded. I read out a prepared statement. There was an immediate acknowledgement that this was for real – the phoney war was over; this was a direct breach of the NBA and the Publishers' Association must respond, otherwise the agreement was dead. The position of Smith's was rightly seen to be crucial. The story featured on every news bulletin on all the radio and television channels throughout the day.

I called the editors of each of the major national newspapers and Simon Jenkins of *The Times* in particular was, as he always has been, specially encouraging. The following day, in addition to the prominent front-page news stories, there were supportive leaders in *The Times*, the *Daily Telegraph*, the *Independent*, and the *Daily Mail*.

I was interviewed for each of the television news channels and at one stage I had three BBC reporters outside my office from different radio programmes within the BBC each wishing to ask almost identical questions and receive almost identical answers – but apparently it was important that each had his own 'exclusive' interview.

The *Sunday Times* was planning a major news feature and Brian MacArthur, who was to write it, had been shadowing the build-up to the campaign for the past week. He was to remain closely in touch with me as events unfolded right up until the final edition deadline at eight o'clock on Saturday evening. Elsewhere, however, things were suddenly not going so well – the publishers were beginning to crumble. I was on the telephone most of Friday afternoon talking to journalists; several told me that they believed that the publishers were to take legal action. At the same time Julian, who had been speaking to his contacts in the publishing houses, told me that he had heard that Collins were considering proceedings. I immediately called Nigel Newton at Bloomsbury as I thought that he was most likely to let me know what was happening. He said that the Publishers' Association had told him that all the other publishers were going to join in legal proceedings and that, as he had always made clear, he could not stand alone as he could not afford to run the risk of retaliatory action from those book retailers who supported the NBA. I asked Nigel to hold his hand whilst I made further enquiries. I spoke to Matthew Evans at Faber who told a similar story; the Publishers' Association had told *him* that all other publishers were supporting legal proceedings and Matthew repeated Nigel's cry that he could not run the risk of being isolated – he needed the comfort of other larger publishers. Matthew also told me that he had been called by another bookseller who had said that if Faber did not join in legal proceedings then they would return all Faber titles. I told Matthew that the publishers were being manipulated by the Publishers' Association who were misrepresenting the true position and were playing one publisher off against another. I then thought it time I called Clive Bradley, the chief executive of the Publishers' Association.

Clive Bradley was a barrister who had once worked for the Labour Party and had stood in its cause, unsuccessfully, as a candidate in a parliamentary by-election. He was a loquacious man who never used one word if two would do. He had been chief executive of the Publishers' Association since 1976. Clive and I were seen in the book trade to be deadly enemies – which was something of an overstatement, and we have developed over the years a reasonably civilised relationship. Our first meeting, some years earlier, had not been an auspicious start. I had received a call from Clive; he had to see me on important and urgent business. I did not know him but we arranged to meet. He came to my office and straightaway told me that the shareholders' discount scheme which Pentos had recently introduced was in breach of the NBA as it allowed shareholders to purchase books from Dillons at less than the cover price. The NBA did not stand high in my thoughts at that time and it had never entered my mind when putting forward the proposals for the shareholders' discount scheme. Nonetheless, it was an early example of its lunacies, since technically Clive was correct. He instructed me in a formal and pompous manner that we must withdraw the Pentos shareholders' scheme immediately. I told him not to be so ridiculous – it was the last thing we were going to do; shareholders were the owners of the business; and did he believe that independent bookshop owners paid the full price for their personal book purchases? He left in a state of high excitement with the threat that he would be taking it further. That took the form of a call from Ian Chapman, who was then President of the Publishers' Association; he asked me to join him for a drink and a chat at his office in St James's. It was all very unfortunate that the scheme had been introduced without consultation, he said, but he could see the embarrassment which would now be caused by its withdrawal. The shareholders' discount scheme continued.

When Clive Bradley came to the telephone he was wary. I told him that I was seriously concerned by threats from other book retailers to publishers which were a breach of competition law; I also said that it was remarkable that publishers who had been generally supportive in the morning appeared to have made such a dramatic U-turn by the afternoon; I considered that they had been subject to improper pressure and manipulation. Clive insisted that he was merely doing his job in administering the NBA – as he believed that the NBA had to be defended at all costs, I suppose he was right. However, I hoped that, as a result of my call, he would be a little more careful.

I got back to re-contacting the publishers. I tried Anthony Cheetham but was told he had left the office and was unavailable; I talked to Eddie Bell who sounded considerably chastened and said that, under the NBA, Collins had no alternative but to support proceedings, though he agreed not to do anything until Monday when we would speak again; I spoke to Nigel Newton and suggested he call Matthew Evans so that they could judge the extent to which the Publishers' Association were misrepresenting the situation and hopefully give each other comfort. I then took a call from the BBC who told me that all the publishers had agreed to support injunction proceedings. I again rang Matthew Evans and he said that this was nonsense; he confirmed that he would not be contactable in any circumstances by others, although he gave me his home telephone number so that we could consult together over the weekend if necessary. I left for my London home in the early evening and as soon as I got in I received a call from Anthony Cheetham. Anthony said that he had deliberately left his office at half past three having spoken to each of the other publishers. He said that the publishers were somewhat put out by the fact that we had taken unilateral action without prior consultation. I thought that this was a bit rich given the recent history and the sheer impossibility of getting the publishers to agree to do anything together. I explained to him that I thought unilateral action was inevitable in the circumstances and that prior consultation would simply have meant that the Publishers' Association would have clanked into gear that much more quickly, and would have increased the risk of retaliatory action from Smith's. Anthony then said that the publishers had agreed that they would all stand together and that they would not proceed to injunct us. That, he said, had been the position when he left his office; however, he had just heard that this understanding had fallen apart, although he did not know the reasons why. I pressed Anthony to speak to Matthew Evans in an attempt to regain control of the situation. Anthony called back within the half-hour; he had not spoken to Matthew but he had spoken to the Publishers' Association and it had been agreed that nothing would happen until Monday, at which time the publishers would meet to discuss the matter further. It seemed we had gained a breathing space and I left in high spirits for the BBC TV Centre where I was to appear on *Newsnight*. Mordecai Richler had been drafted to debate the NBA with me in a live interview. I met him just prior to the performance and it was obvious his heart was not in it. On the programme he virtually conceded the argument; as we left he said, 'Carmen [Carmen Calill, his publisher] will kill me.'

On the Saturday morning, I went into my office and rang Nigel Newton at his home. There were happy family noises in the background but he was clearly distressed. He said Bloomsbury was under enormous pressure. He reminded me of his recent 'run-in' with Waterstone's, the Smith's subsidiary, with regard to terms of trade, which had been very damaging to his young company. He could not suffer a similar situation again. He believed as a result of his conversations with the Publishers' Association that he was isolated. I told him that I did not believe this to be true and that it was misrepresentation by the Publishers' Association to apply pressure. I again urged him to speak to Matthew Evans. It was agreed that whatever happened there would be no action before Monday.

I then visited our central London bookshops to see at first hand how the promotion was going – they were packed. I was driven home to the country and fitted in a late-afternoon game of tennis; at half past five I was called to the telephone. It was our company secretary who was liaising with our lawyers; he told me that the publishers were about to make an application for an injunction. I called Matthew Evans at the number he had given me; the telephone was answered by Caroline Michel (now Mrs Matthew Evans) who was very guarded. She said that I was the only person from whom Matthew was taking calls. When he came to the telephone, he said that he had no knowledge of any proceedings. At about the same time, at approximately quarter past six, lawyers for the Publishers' Association, acting for Collins, Chatto (the Random Century subsidiary) and Bloomsbury, were at the home of Mr Justice Saville. They were making an ex parte application for an interlocutory injunction to prevent Dillons from continuing to sell the titles concerned at lower prices; Mr Justice Saville, as we had been led to expect, granted the injunction, which had immediate effect. There were no lawyers or other representatives of Dillons present and we did not have an opportunity to present any arguments. It later turned out that the only reason that Faber were not party to the original application was because of the technicality that they were not prepared to provide a cross-undertaking in damages; the following week, all six of the Booker titles were no longer on sale at the discounted prices.

The final scene of this particular act is set in the Guildhall, on the following Tuesday, October 16, as the Booker Prize dinner was being held. This annual dinner at which the winner is announced and the awards granted is, in addition to being a literary event, a major public relations opportunity for Booker plc – quite properly as they are footing the bill. So, at dinner, a guest is as likely to be sitting next to a banker or stockbroker as to some literary figure; all this is described a little unflatteringly in Malcolm Bradbury's book *Doctor Criminale*. The only publishers automatically invited are those who have published the shortlisted titles; so I expected to meet my protagonists of the previous week.

As I entered the reception, I first saw Eddie Bell; I then saw Nigel Newton who quickly left his group to come over and tell me in a concerned but friendly way that he would be writing to me to explain what had happened. The always-gregarious Matthew Evans was unabashed and insisted that we join them at the Faber party at the Groucho Club after the dinner – which we did. I saw Anthony Cheetham after the presentations when he was basking in the glory of being the publisher of the winning title; he said that he would be sending a 'billet doux'. The promised letters never arrived; but by then I have no doubt that legal constraints would have made it difficult for them to be sent.

A final point from the dinner: Sir Michael Caine, Booker's chairman, traditionally makes a brief speech before the presentations. He suffers from a speech impediment so it is an act of some courage that he makes a speech at all – but he keeps it short. So it required a major effort on his part to add to his speech some comment on the previous few days. He described the NBA in terms which made clear his feelings on the matter; he referred approvingly to the Dillons Booker promotion; and he said that he was delighted that I was present at the dinner as one of their guests. At the mention of my name there was some, muted, polite applause which was quickly overtaken by stronger booing from a table which included

Tim Waterstone and which, I was told by other guests on the table, he high-spiritedly orchestrated. All good fun – however, it enabled newspapers to refer to 'the man who was booed at the Booker', which is not quite the whole story.

It is astonishing that four publishers, each of whom opposed the NBA with varying degrees of hostility, should have acted as they did. It is remarkable that they should have gone back on what they said to me: each of them had said, at the very least, that there would be no action until Monday; and yet three joined in proceedings on the Saturday and the only reason the fourth did not was because of a technical issue. So long as the publishers had the courage to stick together, the Booker shortlist was an ideal opportunity of dealing a fatal blow to the NBA. As it is, the death throes have continued for more than three more years; which has been divisive for the trade and which has continued to be an obstacle to, and a distraction from, the opportunities of marketing books in a more effective and professional manner. I have some sympathy for Bloomsbury and Faber: small publishing houses which are particularly vulnerable to discriminatory action from other booksellers. I have less sympathy for Random Century, which if it had been more determined and decisive could, I believe, have carried the day. I have no sympathy at all for Collins, which, I believe, was mainly responsible for the capitulation. Dillons had, nevertheless, achieved a number of important objectives from the Booker campaign. It had secured a major public relations coup, and Julian Rivers was later to calculate that the overall media coverage was equivalent to an advertising spend of several millions of pounds; we had obtained further hard evidence to show the value of focused price-led promotions in attracting more customers into bookshops and in selling more books (around seven times as many of the discounted titles were sold than would have been the case without the promotion, and again more than 50 per cent of those buying a promoted title also purchased on average more than two other books); and we had demonstrated to a wider public the iniquities of the net book agreement. We retired to prepare for the next assault.

There have been many false dawns in this long-drawn-out saga. The timing of the end of the NBA has been predicted with various degrees of certainty by participants (including me) and informed commentators as 'a matter of months', 'by the end of the year', and then 'the following year', and yet incredibly it is still with us, though in a weakened state. There is no doubt, however, that the Booker discount promotion was a watershed; within six months one of the three major British publishing groups had withdrawn its support from the NBA and the Publishers' Association, and was publishing all of its titles non-net; things were never to be the same again.

At the beginning of 1991, Dillons, for the third successive year, approached all the major publishers to seek their co-operation for a major promotional offensive (including for the first time national television advertising) planned for the summer of that year; some of them were feeling a little shamefaced in the aftermath of the Booker legal action. Suddenly, the climate seemed quite different. We were told of an informal meeting of the Publishers' Association in early March at which most of the major publishing companies present resolved that during this year they would move to non-net a number of new bestselling titles of literary fiction; a rumoured change of policy by W.H. Smith was said to have been influential. Good news, although in competition law a decision made in concert and in response to a perceived change of stance by the largest retailer in the book trade should have caused some concern to Sir Gordon Borrie. Richard Charkin from Reed (which encompassed literary imprints such as Secker and Warburg, Methuen and Heinemann, as well as Octopus) wrote to Julian Rivers on March 12, 'We support the concept of non-net books in the book trade and we wish to develop a marketing programme with as much haste as possible.' And Ian Irvine had, the previous day, written to me to say, 'I believe that the proposals that are now in place for this summer are likely to give everyone an opportunity to deal with the ending of the NBA in a structured way. Let us hope so anyway' – somewhat different from his last letter to me of almost exactly a year before. Anthony Cheetham had already written a letter to me on January 10 in which he said, 'I understand your frustration over the delays in our introducing the non-net promotion which we have been discussing for the last two years. I think that I have made it quite clear to you where my own sympathies lie but at the same time I will also stress that I can only act if I have a consensus of agreement from my senior colleagues here'; and, 'Once the decision is made I am determined that it should be implemented and not a subject of further prevarication or delay.'

The news seeped into the press. The *Sunday Times* ran a story on March 31 in which it announced, a little prematurely, the end of 'a cartel that has dominated the book trade for more than a century'. Simon Master, deputy chairman of Random Century, was quoted as saying 'some experimentation is going to happen', and Eddie Bell of Collins that 'although we have supported it strongly in the past, I am no longer sure it is valid'.

As quickly as the pendulum had swung in one direction, it was now to swing with equal force in the other.

Independent booksellers orchestrated by the Booksellers' Association expressed highly vocal and emotional opposition to the proposed experimentation (shades of the run-up to the Resale Prices Act 1964) ahead of their annual conference at the end of April; and Sir Simon Hornby, chairman of W.H. Smith, gave an interview in which he expressed his total support for the NBA; either the earlier signals from Smith's had been misread, or there had been a further change of heart, or (to my mind more likely) Sir Simon had re-established his personal views over those of his colleagues. We were told that copies of Sir Simon's interview were circulated by Smith's to major publishers with an implicit warning not to proceed with their de-netting plans.

On April 25, Julian Rivers received a letter from Simon Master at Random Century in which he said, 'We are not willing to join your proposed summer discounting campaign, we have now also abandoned consideration of any plans for selective non-netting of titles in the autumn.' As Julian said in his reply, 'Your letter obviously surprised me a great deal . . . particularly in light of Anthony's [Cheetham's] letter to Terry Maher of 10th January . . . it is impossible for us to construct a campaign in consultation with publishers, if publishers individually, and now collectively, repeatedly make 180 degree turns.' Given the tone of Simon's letter and the lack of even a whiff of an apology, Julian's irritation and frustration were understandable. On May 1, speaking to the Booksellers' Association Conference in Cardiff, Eddie Bell also announced a complete about-turn. He said that, although HarperCollins (as they were now called) had been in favour of a limited experiment with de-netting, he had been persuaded by booksellers' arguments to support the NBA and, therefore, it would not go ahead with its non-net promotion. Only Reed remained; but they were to stay firm.

I have made much of the power and influence of W.H. Smith; and of how they have not been shy of using their muscle when and where it mattered. There are some who feel that I might have exaggerated this. That is certainly the view of Sir Simon Hornby, who, in October 1991, had Smith's lawyers write to me claiming that comments of mine had been defamatory; the matter was not pressed. What is the evidence?

Publishers large and small were always, in my experience, extremely careful not to take any action which might offend W.H. Smith, their largest customer. There was an exception in the early part of 1991 when several publishers made a public stand against a unilateral, and it was thought unreasonable, demand by Smith's for improved terms. But this was a defensive move rather than an initiative for change; and it was very much the exception undertaken with great reluctance and trepidation. It could be argued that all this is no more than the small change of everyday business life; retailers are always seeking a better deal from their suppliers; and suppliers, if they are to stay in business, will be concerned not to upset their customers gratuitously – particularly their most important one. Those who have read Marcus Sieff's memoirs, *Don't Ask the Price*, will know that Marks and Spencer can be tough with suppliers who do not toe the line. However, with Smith's I believe it was more than this; and with the competition law implications of their dominant market position (they have between 27 per cent and 30 per cent of the UK retail book market) and of the NBA they had to be doubly careful.

Publishers in their discussions with Dillons executives on pursuing legitimate sales opportunities within the existing law were paranoid about the likely response of Smith's to any proposed initiative. It was difficult to have a meeting without an awareness of its unseen presence. And we had seen that, when it came to a frontal attack on the NBA with the Booker promotion, Smith's executives were not slow to spell out the implications of support for Dillons' position – publishers, rightly or wrongly, perceived a situation in which large numbers of books would be returned. I believe the experience of Reed's, however, to be conclusive. After the sudden desertion of Random Century and HarperCollins, Reed were left to stand alone in their commitment to leave the NBA.

In June I saw Peter Davis, Reed's chief executive, at a charity reception at 10 Downing Street. He took me to one side to say, 'The two knights [Sir Simon Hornby and Sir Malcolm Field, Smith's managing director] have asked to see me about you know what.' The meeting took place some two weeks later and in the event the delegation consisted of Sir Malcolm Field and Tim Waterstone. I do not know what transpired at the meeting, but I am fairly confident that Smith's will have been extremely careful to keep well within the bounds of what is allowed under our competition laws. However, the perception of an implied threat remained. Peter Davis is the chief executive of an enormous company of which the consumer books side, although large in the book trade, was a comparatively small part. He would not normally be involved in its day-to-day affairs. The insistence upon a meeting with him can only have been to ensure that he was fully aware of the possible implications for Reed as a whole (Smith's was also Reed's largest customer for its important consumer magazine business) of its proposed move on the NBA. In the event Smith's bluff was called; but there are not many in the book trade who have the resources to be so courageous. There was a sequel. On September 27 (coincidentally, the same day as Dillons' latest and biggest promotional blast against the NBA), I was invited to lunch at 11 Downing Street where I found that Peter Davis was a fellow guest. As we sat down to lunch, the Chancellor of the Exchequer, Norman Lamont, who was our host, straightaway turned to me and to my surprise asked me what was happening to the NBA. Before I could reply, Peter Davis intervened to say, with feeling, 'Tell him, Terry, that the only reason we still have a net book agreement is because of W.H. Smith.'

Still, there are those who say, 'But, surely, Smith's would be the biggest beneficiary if the net book agreement were to go.' That is certainly what Smith's publicly claim. They argue, unconvincingly, that they support the agreement because it protects small, independent bookshops, preserves diversity in the range of books which are published, and actually keeps prices down. Their shareholders must then be astonished to hear them say that they hold to this position despite the fact that they would gain market share and improve their profitability if the agreement were to go. The whistle was blown on Smith's by Tim Coates, the former managing director of their specialist bookshop chain Sherratt and Hughes and Waterstone's. He wrote to the trade press to say that it was common knowledge within Smith's that the reason for their stance on the NBA was fear of the supermarkets becoming more active in book retailing in a freer and more competitive market. That has long been my view. I believe that, following the abolition of the NBA, the specialist chains offering range and authority such as Dillons and Waterstone's (and also the better independents) will do well; that supermarkets and other non-traditional book retailers will be drawn more into bookselling, offering a limited range of bestselling titles, particularly at times such as Christmas; and that Smith's run the risk of being squeezed. I believe that this will increase the availability and accessibility of books to a wider public; which will be good for the book trade and for literacy and, as it so happens, for Dillons.

Smith's chairman, Sir Simon Hornby, has identified himself personally with the retentionist case, and it was not always clear that his views had enthusiastic backing in the lower ranks; it seemed to some, at least, that Smith's had got themselves painted into a corner in supporting a not very popular or consumer-friendly line. The media, who in any event love to personalise these things, had long portrayed the battle as being between Sir Simon and me. Despite this, as Peter Gorb at the London Business School established, we had never actually debated together in public. At his invitation we both agreed to a debate at the Business School under the chairmanship of its principal Professor George Bain.

On November 20, we met in George's office half an hour before the debate to discuss the procedure. Over the past three years I had debated this issue on a number of occasions with different people and it had always been assumed that as I was proposing abolition I should speak first. I had never challenged this, although the logic seemed doubtful and I believed that there was an advantage in speaking second. On this occasion I suggested that we spin a coin to decide the batting order and that is what George did. I called correctly and then stupidly said, 'I'll speak first.' As soon as the words were out I realised I had said the wrong thing – but it was too late. It was agreed that I would propose abolition; Simon would oppose; two senior academic economists from the

Business School would then speak, one, Professor David Currie, in support of me, and one, Professor John Kay, in support of Simon; there would be contributions from the floor after which Simon and I would sum up. It was George Bain's idea that the speaking order should be reversed at the end of the debate, which meant that I was in the unexpected but fortunate position of having the last word. We then discussed whether we should have a vote. I had seen the list of those who had said they were to attend and of the names I recognised there were many of the book trade establishment. I said cheerfully that I was happy to have a vote but that I thought the result was a forgone conclusion as a fair proportion of those attending would have their minds set and were unlikely to be swayed by debate. George suggested a vote before and after so that we could determine how the debate had influenced opinion. Simon thought we should keep it simple and just vote at the end – which is what we decided.

The debating hall was packed, and amongst the crowd were Sir Gordon Borrie and his officials from the Office of Fair Trading. I made what were by now my standard debating points that the NBA prevents us from exploiting the full potential for expanding book sales; has kept book prices unnecessarily high; and has propped up widespread inefficiencies in the book trade. I also developed the theme of 'quality not quantity'. The defenders of the NBA insist that its abolition will mean that fewer books will be published. There is no factual support for this argument (indeed the impact of secondary purchases should mean more sales of all types of books across the range, not just bestsellers) but I pointed out that there are many in the book trade who believe, in any event, that 60,000 new titles each year is too many and that there was a danger of a form of Gresham's law applying to books; there was a risk of bad books driving out good books; good books very often do not get the attention they deserve and do not stay in print as long as they should. For his part Simon trotted out the standard NBA defence: its abolition will mean fewer books, higher prices, fewer bookshops. He also placed great stress on Smith's user-friendly image with publishers. Smith's, he argued, worked in close co-operation with publishers for the general good of the book trade, and he contrasted this with what he described, with a little justification, as Dillons' more confrontational approach. There were a number of lively contributions from the floor. The most telling, I thought, was from a past president of the American Booksellers' Association. The competitive, free market environment of the US book trade had, he said, 'improved the calibre of booksellers. It forces those who don't want to compete on price to compete on other offerings.' Then there were the rebuttals. When it came to my turn, I enjoyed the unplanned-for benefits of the last word. I was able to destroy Simon's description of Smith's cosy and constructive relationship with publishers by reminding him of its run-in with a number of major publishers earlier in the year when Smith's had sought to impose improved trading terms; the publishers had taken the unprecedented step of suspending supplies. Simon, scion of Smith's founding families, was most unamused; he was used to a more deferential manner than this. I concluded my attack on the NBA, not very originally, by repeating Leo Amery's message to Neville Chamberlain in 1940, 'In the name of God, go.'

At the end, a show of hands was inconclusive, and the chairman declared a draw. Sir Gordon Borrie and his colleagues abstained. George Bain was to tell me at a later date that he believed virtually all of those who were uncommitted at the outset had voted for abolition; and Gordon Graham wrote to me to say, 'But the main achievement was yours, in getting about 50 per cent support from an audience which, a few years ago, would not have elected, or in some cases dared, to disapprove of the net book agreement.'

In June 1991 a letter of support arrived, out of the blue, from an unlikely source. It was from Christina Foyle, and in her own hand. It was prompted by a profile of me in the *Sunday Telegraph*. She said that I reminded her of her 'beloved father'. This, from a lady in her eighties, was doubtful praise. She went on to say, 'We have a good deal in common. I hate the net book agreement, and I spent nearly all my childhood in sanatoriums with tuberculosis. Even today, I can't add up.' An invitation followed for the next Foyle's literary lunch. Christina Foyle has been organising regular literary lunches for almost seventy years. They are an established part of the London scene and in that enormous time-span Christina has met most of the significant figures of the century. Indeed, I can think of nobody who has met as many important and interesting people. She is a diminutive, lively person, full of mischief and full of anecdotes. I sat next to her at my first Foyle's lunch and she regaled me with stories about events and people – but mainly people. She told me that she had the most enormous collection of letters and that one was from Hitler. She explained that she had been concerned at the time to read in the newspapers that Hitler and his henchmen in Germany were burning books. She wrote to him to say that if he wished to be rid of the books why not send them to her for her shop and she would make a contribution to his funds. He apparently replied that he would not do that as he was equally anxious not to corrupt the youth of Britain. I heard the story in horrified silence as she told it with a straight face, but with perhaps the usual hint of mischief in her eyes. I was later invited to lunch at Christina's home at Beeleigh Abbey. For many years she has come up to London only one day a week and the administrative side of the bookshop is run from the Abbey. I asked her how she got on with publishers. She said straightaway: 'Oh, I never see publishers – I leave that to the shop manager.' She justified the tortuous process required to purchase books from her Charing Cross Road shop on the grounds that the American tourists liked it that way and she was not going to change it now. After each subsequent initiative on the NBA, I would receive a further letter from Christina urging me not to give up the struggle; 'it will help the book trade all over the country,' she would exclaim. And there was always an amusing aside. She remarked on the fact that we were cutting the price of both Mother Teresa and Madonna and then went on to say, 'Once, coming home from abroad, and going through customs, the man next to me was asked if he had any pornography; he said: "I haven't even got a pornograph."'

On September 27, 1991, Dillons launched the latest of its 'lower book prices' promotions. The price of more than twenty leading new titles was reduced by 25 per cent. It was the most powerful promotion so far. Reed's defection from the net book agreement meant that new novels by authors such as David Lodge and Roddy Doyle, both published by the Reed imprint Secker and Warburg, could be included in the promotion. We also included four net titles from other publishers to test further the resolve of the Publishers' Association. The response was swift, and the following day an injunction was obtained preventing Dillons from selling the four 'offending' titles at the lower price. The offer remained an impressive one, however, and for the first time was supported by extensive national television advertising. The provocation of David Lodge's *Paradise News* being offered at £11.20 rather than £14.99 during the advertising break on the *South Bank Show* was too much for the competition. Within days Smith's specialist bookselling chain Waterstone's had followed suit; Books Etc., a London-based chain, was next. This new development looked set to bring more pressure to bear on the NBA. But it was soon to fizzle out. Waterstone's and Books Etc.'s hearts really were not in it; they had responded in haste if not in panic and the implications had not been thought through. Point-of-sale material was poor and advertising support non-existent. Visits to their shops exposed rather sorry-looking displays compared to the professional and highly visible window and in-store displays with banners, headers, and showcards at Dillons. If you are launching a price promotion you must tell your customers about it – as aggressively as possible; and this they failed to do. They retired hurt, claiming the experiment to be a failure.

Dillons' results were far from a failure, but followed a similar pattern to previous promotions; on this occasion the figures were independently verified by Coopers and Lybrand to silence any sceptics; and there had been the by now usual blanket media coverage. (The inclusion of Alex Comfort's new book in the promotion meant that headline writers had great fun with 'Joy of Sex reduced by 25 per cent'.)

Price-led promotions, featuring a number of new hardback titles, including literary fiction, were now a regular feature of Dillons' marketing programme. They were an effective way of drawing more people into bookshops and, as we never tired of explaining, once people are in bookshops they do buy books. Reed's withdrawal from the NBA had made these promotions possible; but Reed titles accounted for only a small proportion of the total number of new titles published in Britain each year and so our offer was still severely restricted in its appeal; and the vast array of marketing techniques which are available to other retailers (often selling products which compete with books) were still not available to booksellers. Early in 1992, Dillons was approached by one of the clearing banks. They were to launch a major national television advertising programme which would be targeting children between the ages of eleven and sixteen. They wanted to offer shopping concessions at Dillons as an inducement; those opening a new account would be given vouchers exchangeable in Dillons bookstores for books. We had to explain to the disbelieving agency acting for the bank that the restrictions of the NBA would not allow Dillons to participate; so an opportunity to bring new young customers into bookshops and to get them into the habit of regular bookbuying was lost – possibly to McDonald's. We have had to respond similarly to the many other third-party sponsors who would like to be associated with the cultural values which books represent; and the same restrictions have prevented Dillons from introducing customer loyalty and other specific discount cards which are commonplace in other forms of retailing and which are also used by booksellers in other countries.

In September 1990, Dillons had introduced a student voucher scheme. New students, at the start of term, were given £1 vouchers redeemable at Dillons. We thought it little different from free credit offered by other booksellers, but, nonetheless, it was quickly squashed by the threat of legal action from the Publishers' Association. In October 1991, a new voucher scheme was introduced as a top-up to the promotion which had started the previous month. Bookbuyers obtained the voucher with each promoted non-net title they purchased (in addition to the 25 per cent discount), and it was then redeemable on all other books, including net books. The scheme had been drawn up in close consultation with our lawyers to ensure that this time it did not fall foul of the NBA (despite the fact that we were of course advised that the agreement had no legal effect because of the European judgement – which the UK courts had yet to concede), and it ran almost to Christmas when it was withdrawn so as to avoid a further and by then unnecessary legal confrontation. However, an important side-issue provided a further example of the lengths to which the Publishers' Association were prepared to go, and of the risks which publishers ran in taking the Association's advice. Although the vouchers were generally redeemable against net books, we had felt it prudent to make one exception. We were concerned, despite the strong, positive legal advice, not to take even the remotest risk of breaching a Court Order. We had therefore established with our lawyers a strict compliance programme in all our bookshops to ensure that, so far as possible, none of the specific books subject to injunctions was included in the voucher scheme. The procedures were stringent and detailed and were in accordance with principles which had been established by the Court of Appeal (the precedent for those who are interested is *Director General of Fair Trading* v. *Smiths Concrete Ltd*). Given the existence of such a programme, an innocent mistake by one of Dillons' staff would not incur any liability. Dillons' lawyers kept the lawyers acting for the Publishers' Association fully informed of the implementation of the compliance programme. Despite this, and without any consultation or prior notification, the Publishers' Association issued a press release on October 22, 1991, claiming a breach of the Court Order by Dillons in allowing the vouchers to be used against the purchase of injuncted titles and announcing action to enforce the injunction by a motion for committal and sequestration of assets. They were trying to have me put in gaol. Up until now, we had been irritated and frustrated by the Publishers' Association but had recognised, if reluctantly, that they had a job to do. But now there was real anger. That anger was to grow as the full involvement of the Association's officers became clear. The chief executive of the Publishers' Association and the personal assistant of its then President had visited separate Dillons bookstores and, in complicated transactions, had purchased a number of books including an injuncted title; they had acted as agents provocateurs. I immediately contacted the three publishers on whose behalf the Association had claimed to be acting: Faber and Faber, Sinclair-Stevenson and Random Century. Matthew Evans said that he was outraged by the press release from the Publishers' Association and that 'we are not going to be a party to contempt proceedings and I am going to tell Clive Bradley so'; in a separate telephone call he told me that his colleague Brigid MacLeod had agreed to join the proceedings on the mistaken assumption that they were no more than the continuation of the injunctive proceedings.

Christopher Sinclair-Stevenson came to my office at noon, and made clear his extreme unease; whilst we were talking, Matthew telephoned again to say that Faber had formally withdrawn. Christopher told me that he would think very seriously about the position and telephone me in the afternoon. The issue was less straightforward for Christopher; his company was new and vulnerable (it is now part of Reed Consumer Books), it supported the net book agreement, and a fellow director and major shareholder was Dillons' arch-rival Tim Waterstone. Nonetheless, he telephoned in mid-afternoon to say that Sinclair-Stevenson would withdraw.

Random Century was a little more difficult to pin down. I had telephoned Anthony Cheetham the previous morning to discuss a different aspect of the proceedings. I was told that he was in a board meeting, but at about half past eleven he returned my call to tell me that he was about to leave Random Century; I asked him if it was his idea and he said no (he has now founded the publishing house Orion). So, on the morning of the 'contempt of court' press release, I sought to speak to the new head of Random Century, Gail Rebuck. Perhaps not surprisingly in the circumstances, she was rather elusive and more inclined to rely on the Publishers' Association and its lawyers. After an exchange of faxed letters, however, Simon Master telephoned to say that he was speaking in the presence of Gail and that, having now been acquainted with the facts, they were about to instruct the Publishers' Association to withdraw Jonathan Cape (the Random Century imprint) from the proceedings.

There was now total capitulation. The Publishers' Association, on behalf of the publishers involved, sought and was granted leave by the court on November 1, 1991 to withdraw its actions and its allegations of contempt of court; it accepted the adequacy of Dillons' compliance system; and it agreed to pay Dillons' costs. The action was both misconceived and mischievous. It ended in a small victory for Dillons but it was a shabby episode and it left a nasty taste.

That was, to my knowledge, the last time the NBA was brought before the UK courts, and the spotlight switched to Europe. The European Commission had ruled in December 1988 that the UK NBA was incompatible with the competition policy provision of the Treaty of Rome. The Publishers' Association appealed to the European Court of Justice against the Commission's ruling and in July 1992 the Court of First Instance dismissed the appeal and ordered the applicant to pay the costs. A further appeal has now been lodged by the Publishers' Association with the European Court of Appeal, which is the final arbiter on the matter. All of the legal actions brought against Dillons by the Publishers' Association, on behalf of its members, have been referred by the UK courts to the European Court where they rest pending the final outcome of the appeal process. So, although injunctions have been granted against Dillons by the UK courts, the substantive issues have not been tested in court, and the court has not ruled on the continuing validity of the NBA. Dillons' consistent legal advice has been that the agreement ceased to be enforceable in the UK Court of Law with the Commission's decision of December 1988. Five and a half years later, justice is still awaited. It is not a good example for those who look to Europe for a lead.

There was an important change at the Office of Fair Trading in May 1992 when Sir Gordon Borrie retired as Director General and was replaced by Sir Bryan Carsberg. Sir Gordon and Sir Bryan have similar professional backgrounds, but they are quite different personalities. Sir Gordon is a lawyer who had practised at the Bar but who had then made his reputation as an academic; he was Professor of Law at the University of Birmingham until he went to the Office of Fair Trading in 1976; he had been an unsuccessful Labour candidate in the 1955 and 1959 elections. Sir Bryan is a chartered accountant who after two years in private practice also became an academic, being Professor of Accounting at the University of Manchester and at the London School of Economics; he had then made an impact as Director General of Telecommunications (the industry regulatory body) until in 1992 he took up his appointment as Director General of Fair Trading. Sir Gordon is bow-tied, extrovert, fluent and very much the advocate; Sir Bryan is small, precise, lucid and very determined.

I wrote to Sir Bryan, in his first months in his new office, urging him to reconsider Sir Gordon's 1989 decision not to take the question of the NBA back to the Restrictive Practices Court. I told him of developments since 1989: the further sharp increase in real terms in book prices; the withdrawal of Reed from the NBA; and, most importantly, the absence of the promised Government legislation on restrictive practices, the expectation of which had been so influential in forming Sir Gordon's decision not to refer. We had a meeting with Sir Bryan and his officials at the end of September and I was immediately of the view that his approach was likely to be quite different from that of his predecessor. Sir Gordon, at one of our meetings, had said to me that he was an agnostic on the issue of the net book agreement but that, in any event, his personal opinion was of no consequence as his role was simply to administer the law. Whilst I was sure that Sir Bryan would be equally scrupulous in his approach to the administration of the law, I was also certain that he did not think much of the NBA and, as he had for several years been a director of the Economist Bookshops when they were partly owned by the London School of Economics (they are now owned by Dillons), he had first-hand experience of the book trade. It seemed to me that he was concerned to establish the most efficient method (in terms of time and cost) of securing a judicial review; and that if the Government would not act then he would. I continued to keep his office abreast of developments in the book trade and wrote to Sir Bryan finally on August 4, 1993. I drew his attention to further changes in book club regulations; to a recent move of book clubs into high street retailing; and to a change in the rules governing the NBA which had been introduced to allow W.H. Smith to operate a particular promotional scheme. All of these changes brought about further distortions of competition in the book market. I argued that 'not only is the net book agreement an agreement in restraint of trade and operating against the public interest, it is also administered in an arbitrary way and partisan manner to favour particular distribution channels and particular booksellers. We believe that we [Dillons] suffer significant economic loss as a result', and concluded, 'In view of this new evidence we hope that you will feel able to make some public statement on the matter. Whilst we recognise the delay involved in a reference to the Restrictive Practices Court we believe the weight of evidence would justify a reference if there is no more expedite alternative. We are of course still awaiting proposals from the Government to reform the restrictive trade practices legislation.' Sir Bryan replied on August 24, 'I am not yet ready to comment publicly on the matter you mentioned.'

On November 23, after the Queen's Speech on the forthcoming legislative programme, the Director General of Fair Trading announced that the NBA was to be re-examined. He explained: 'The agreement would have come up for review as a matter of course after enactment of the Government's proposals for new legislation prohibiting anti-competition agreements. Unfortunately, the Government has been unable to find time to introduce a bill covering these proposals this session. I consider, therefore, that I should review the case under existing legislation, in order to decide whether to apply to the Court for leave to have its decision reviewed.'

So the NBA is being re-examined by the Office of Fair Trading; is being considered by the final Court of Appeal in Europe; and has been abandoned by one of the three major British publishing groups. The question must be asked: 'Has it been worth all the effort?' The answer is, without any reservation whatsoever, in the affirmative. Dillons has single-handedly placed the net book agreement on the public agenda. And, although I am no longer prepared to forecast precisely how and when it will meet its demise, there are few inside or outside the book trade who do not believe that its days are numbered. I suppose that I am now less optimistic that the book trade will reform itself, and feel that it will be regulatory action either here or in Europe which will hasten the end. It has taken longer than I had ever thought likely. I had seriously underestimated the enormous energy required to bring about change and the sheer power of inertia. As Machiavelli wrote in *The Prince*, 'the reformer has enemies in all those who profit by the old order and only lukewarm defenders in all those who would profit by the new'. It has, at the same time, been very good for Dillons. The book chain has received the equivalent of millions of pounds' worth of free advertising and it has helped to establish Dillons as Britain's premier bookselling brand. It has cost little in money terms (each promotion was at least self-funding) and has taken less time than this narrative might suggest. The action tended to be packed into a small number of short, sustained bursts, each confined to two or three days, and it was not usually a distraction from mainstream activities. It was good for morale. Dillons staff, almost without exception, identified with the campaign. It was a high-profile and tangible example of Dillons' beliefs in practice; and, together with its increasingly visible and distinctive presence in the high street, of its commitment to its mission of widening the market for books. Finally, and this should not be overlooked, it has been enormous fun.

5

Pentos Battles with Recession

The acquisition of Hatchards and the publication of our results for 1990 were the high-water mark of the Pentos story. The share price, which had fallen to 85p after Black Monday in October 1987, had drifted further to touch a low of 77p in 1989; the rights issue, in a depressed stock market, had been struck at 87p, and the price had subsequently risen to 115p, before rising further to 171p in 1991 after the 1990 results – almost back to the pre-Black Monday all-time high of 184p in the summer of 1987. In the 1991 Pentos annual report, within the mass of statistical data which we always published – we disclosed far more information than most public companies – we were able to state that £10,000 invested in Pentos in January 1972 (when it all started) with dividend and rights entitlement income re-invested, had a market value of £573,000 at December 31, 1991; an investment in the *Financial Times* all share index on the same basis was worth £151,000. There was a perception that Pentos had weathered the recession better than most retailers; and that we had been far-sighted in pressing ahead with our expansion plans through such difficult times. Retailers had suffered particularly badly in this recession, with its special impact on reduced consumer spending (over-borrowed consumers were having to cope with high interest rates at a time when many were losing or in fear of losing their jobs and when the value of their homes had crumbled to produce the new phenomenon of the reverse equity gap) and with the continuing, remorseless increase in shop rental costs. (Retail rents had risen rapidly in the Eighties, in response to increased demand for space from expanding retailers in the midst of a consumer boom; rents were still being jacked-up, typically by 100 per cent, however, at a time of weak demand and a major fall-off in consumer spending, due to the operation of the standard 'institutional' 25-year lease and the 'time-bomb' effect of its upwards-only rent review every five years; the situation was exacerbated by the introduction of the uniform business rate in 1990, which effectively transferred part of the tax burden from non-retail businesses to retailers.) Many retailers, particularly those which had over-expanded in the mid-1980s, had faced difficulties, and these included household names such as Alexon, Body Shop, Burtons, Dixons, Harris Queensway, Laura Ashley, Next, Ratners, Sears, Sock Shop, Storehouse and Tie Rack; most of these have since made a full or partial recovery, but some were overwhelmed by the scale of their problems. I felt that at Pentos we had come through the recession in reasonable shape. In my statement in the 1991 annual report, I said, 'In the midst of the longest and deepest recession since the Second World War, a profit increase of 7 per cent [we had reported profits of £15.2 million] represents a satisfactory outcome for 1991. In particular, Dillons' performance was outstanding'; and concluded, 'It now looks as if the worst of the recession is behind us.' Little did I realise that the worst was yet to come as the monetary screw continued to be senselessly tightened and the recession took its final downwards lurch and entered its most dangerous phase; it was little consolation that we were not alone in our misjudgement, as an increasing debt burden placed us at greater risk; Nemesis was about to appear on the scene, and was lurking in the wings ready to pounce.

If the acquisition of Hatchards and the 1990 results represented the zenith of Pentos's achievements in the judgement of the external assessors in the City, the Wilding purchase and the announcement of the 1991 figures signalled a sea change in stock market sentiment.

Wilding Office Equipment plc was a quoted company which had fallen upon hard times. It had three businesses: it was the leading UK specialist retailer of business machines, particularly personal computers, with 65 shops; it had a direct sales operation selling office equipment; and it was also a manufacturer of office screens and related office furniture under the name Open Plan. Remarkably, like Pentos, it was a specialist retailer with an office furniture subsidiary; it seemed the perfect fit. We first began to look seriously at Wilding when Open Plan was put up for sale and offered to us in the middle of 1991. Its product range filled an acknowledged gap in the Pentos office furniture armoury, and there would be important savings from merging the different manufacturing facilities; Open Plan's freehold factories in Essex could be closed and sold, and its manufacturing operations transferred to our existing facilities in Derbyshire. We looked more closely at Wilding as a whole. Ryman was already a retailer of business machines; it was peripheral to its main stationery offer but it had been identified as an area of greater potential; it was already proposing to experiment with exclusive Ryman business machine shops as it could not offer an adequate service from a small section of an already small Ryman shop. Wilding would enable Ryman to make a quantum leap; it would bring in new expertise, there would be scope for cross-fertilisation of products and ideas within both chains, Wilding's wider geographic spread would complement Ryman's South-East bias, and there would be significant savings from closing Wilding's existing warehouses and offices, and utilising the spare capacity in Ryman's new distribution centre. Ryman's management were understandably excited at the prospects and became the enthusiastic driving force for the deal to be struck.

Wilding had been particularly badly scarred by the recession; it reported a loss of £3 million for the year ended September 30, 1991, and its borrowings had increased to £5.8 million, giving it gearing (borrowings as a percentage of shareholders' funds) of 140 per cent. It was clearly on the brink, and we considered the possibility of waiting to deal with a receiver, but death throes can often be prolonged as well as damaging to the underlying business. On December 16, 1991, we announced an agreed share exchange which valued Wilding at £4 million; in addition, as I was determined that we should not add further to Pentos's borrowings, we again drew on our resources of innovation and repaid Wilding's bank debt of £5.8 million by the issue of further shares in Pentos – a complicated technique under Stock Exchange rules which we were told had not been used before. We then moved quickly to stem Wilding's losses and the associated cash outflow. Within three months, the direct sales operation was sold to its management for £1.1 million in cash, Open Plan's operations were transferred to Derbyshire, and Wilding's retailing activities had been integrated with Ryman.

Everything was not, however, plain sailing. The Open Plan move was not well executed, and its business was unnecessarily disrupted for a number of months, which resulted in a serious decline in service standards and the loss of several customers to competitors; the move still brought about an overall improvement in profitability, but it was not at the level which had been envisaged. We had also underestimated the working capital requirements of the Wilding business machine shops (they were quickly re-badged 'Ryman Computer Store'), despite a full investigation prior to the acquisition by our auditors; it meant an additional strain of several million pounds on our borrowings, which, in the context of our affairs as a whole, was not that material, but it came at the worst possible time. Finally, we had of course misjudged the course of the recession and Wilding's markets were being more severely affected and would take longer to recover than we had assumed. Nonetheless, Wilding and Open Plan made a useful contribution to the Pentos results in 1992 and they were on course to remain profitable in the more difficult market conditions of 1993.

The Wilding acquisition was by no means a disaster, then, and the £10 million consideration, all in shares, with Pentos capitalised at £200 million, was hardly earth-shattering. Its timing, with the benefit of hindsight, had proved to be unfortunate and it now needed more time and the end of the recession to prove its worth. I believed its competitive position, offering expert service and convenience on the high street to customers who were often desperately insecure and computer-illiterate, to be a strong one. Nothing, therefore, prepared us for, or justified, the hostility with which the deal was received and the continued sniping (first from the stockbrokers' retail analysts, and then, following the feeding chain of the City, the financial press and the institutions) which it suffered for the next two years. However, in the short-term time-horizons of the City, perception can be everything, and the received wisdom was that Pentos had made a mistake; it had blotted its copybook.

The 1991 profits of £15.2 million were, as I have already indicated, perfectly respectable; the results announcement was dominated, however, by a debate about reverse premiums. Reverse premiums are payments (inducements) paid by a landlord to a tenant on entering into a new lease. The inducement can also take the form of a rent-free period. As an example, on a property where the proposed rent is £100,000 per annum, the landlord might offer the prospective tenant, on signing a normal twenty-five-year lease, a cash payment of £200,000 or a rent 'holiday' for the first two years; often the proposal would be a combination of both. There is nothing new in any of this, and it has always been a feature of landlord/tenant negotiation; indeed, when property is scarce and tenants are plentiful, the tenant would often find that he had to pay a premium to the landlord. Reverse premiums became more common in the late Eighties and early Nineties as a number of new shopping centres (many of them out-of-town) all came on stream together, at a time when the recession meant that there was less demand for space from retailers. Taking a unit in a new out-of-town shopping centre was a much riskier proposition for a retailer than renting a shop in a conventional high street. Judgements would have to be made as to the likelihood of customers changing their established shopping patterns – how many of them and how long would it take? The retailer would also have to judge when the centre might become fully let, and often, at the time of entering into the lease commitment, he would not know who might be his immediate neighbours. So there are far more uncertainties than in the high street where the adjacencies and the established traffic flow are known. It could often take a new shopping centre several years before it generated sufficient customer flow to justify the rent; reverse premiums or rent-free periods were an essential contribution to the retailer's costs during this period of business development; they certainly did not represent a windfall profit.

Any apparent 'profits' (including reverse premiums) which were associated with retail property transactions were shown separately in our management accounts and were specifically identified in reports to the main Pentos board. John Stuttard, the engagement partner from our auditors Coopers and Lybrand, would each year, at the conclusion of the audit, write a long letter to the board setting out the main issues which had arisen from the audit, and property income would always be a feature; this would then be discussed at a meeting between the auditors and the full board (for the 1992 accounts this was superseded by the audit committee). It was routinely confirmed that property income was an integral part of retail operations; that separate disclosure would be misleading as it would only show one side of the transaction, the other side being the start-up costs of the new shops to which the property income related; and that our policy was consistent – which Coopers confirmed – with other retail companies. The boardroom discussion was mainly between the auditors and the non-executive directors, particularly, prior to the establishment of the audit committee, with Victor Blank; which was of obvious comfort to the auditors and gave added weight to the views of the board as a whole.

As the audit of the 1991 accounts was drawing to a close, John Stuttard suggested to us that we might consider reviewing our accounting policy on reverse premiums. He believed that other retail companies would be looking at their policies, and, as Coopers had a wide range of audit clients including many retailers, we assumed that this was more than inspired guesswork. Because of the timing of year ends (Pentos's year end is December 31), we would be the first retailer to be reporting in 1992, and John believed that we would be given some credit if it could be seen that we had taken the lead in being the first company to make a clear public statement of its accounting policy in this clouded area. We asked Coopers to do some more research on the subject and to come back to us with its conclusions and recommendations. The eventual proposal was that the income from reverse premiums should be spread over two accounting periods rather than one. The reasons for this proposal were that: it more accurately matched costs (including start-up costs) with revenues (the reverse premiums), which is the convention on which accounts should be prepared; it would, on average, be consistent with the accounting treatment of rent-free periods; it was probably a more conservative policy than that followed by many other retailers (the lack of any published information on this subject made this difficult to determine although we assumed that John Stuttard would have had access, without disclosing the source, to the policies of other Coopers clients); and it was obviously more prudent than the existing Pentos policy. The recommendation was accepted by the Pentos board, and when the 1991 results were announced in March 1992 we made a statement about the change in accounting policy.

The usual meeting with stockbrokers' analysts which followed the results announcement was obsessively concentrated on the reverse premiums issue; why had we changed, and what were the amounts involved? The newspapers took up the story from the analysts and a typical headline was 'Pentos accounting change' rather than 'Pentos copes well with recession', which we might more reasonably have expected; not surprisingly, our shareholders were concerned. I explained patiently that to publish the *gross* amount of the reverse premiums and to isolate them from the related start-up costs would be misleading and that the *net* amount was not deemed to be material; the judgement of the Pentos board in this matter was the same as that of every other retailer, none of whom made any disclosure; and, if Pentos alone were to disclose additional information, we would, in stock market terms, be at a competitive disadvantage with other retailers, as analysts, in their often simplistic style, would most likely deduct the *gross* reverse premiums from reported profits, which would not be in the interest of our shareholders. But, like the dance of the seven veils, once the first veil is removed the pressure for the rest to follow is almost irresistible; and analysts do not like to be defied. Almost every piece of research or comment from stockbrokers was focused on the reverse premium issue; and the pack was led by County NatWest who, only a year ago, had published a eulogistic circular on Pentos; now its constant utterances, both in its own material and in the extensive quotes which it gave to newspapers, undermined our credibility. We had made a major blunder. It was another black mark for Pentos; and ironically it was a move towards greater disclosure and a more prudent policy which was responsible; perhaps not surprisingly, despite Coopers' assumed prescience, hardly another retailer was to follow our lead.

The Wilding acquisition and the reverse premium issue now coloured most press comment on Pentos, and the former stock market star was gradually assuming the appearance of a 'dog'. Factors which previously had been viewed as positive were now perceived as negative, such as the pace of our retail expansion and what was seen as my own overly enthusiastic and determined leadership; there was a muttering of an inappropriately dominant 'management style'.

I was certainly a 'hands-on' manager, but I do not believe that I was either dictatorial or autocratic; nor was I a workaholic.

Pentos was organised as a decentralised holding company with a small head office and with authority and responsibility devolved to the operating subsidiaries. In the later years, there were four separate businesses and each had its own board of directors and chief executive (three of whom had worked with me for more than ten years). I chaired the monthly board meeting for each business and the chief executives reported directly to me. In addition to formal discussion at the monthly meetings I would most often see chief executives separately and briefly perhaps once a week and speak with them on the telephone most days; this would vary, however, depending on priorities and the nature of the business; for example, it would be unusual not to speak to Frank Brazier of Dillons on a daily basis, but a week would sometimes go by without a talk with Brian Matthews at Office Furniture. The chief executives had a high degree of authority to act within business plans which would be agreed annually and against which performance was measured on a continuing basis. Monthly management accounts were reviewed by the Pentos finance director and by me and would be discussed at the subsidiary board meeting; consolidated management accounts with a commentary from the finance director were circulated to the main Pentos board each month and were discussed at its two-monthly meetings. Capital projects, for example a new shop, would without exception be initiated by the relevant chief executive, but would require my authorisation above a modest level of expenditure and main board approval at a higher level.

Much of my own time was spent on shop visits which I found as satisfying and constructive as anything I did, although with more than 500 shops it was inevitable that many were overlooked – at least by me. I received detailed sales and bank figures each day and the weekly figures would be telephoned to me at home on Saturday evening. I rarely worked at the weekends, which were mainly spent reading and playing tennis, and which were usually business-free apart from the telephoned sales figures. I took my full five-week holiday entitlement and the skiing weeks were the highlights of the year; the routine daily telephone calls I made to the office and the faxed sales figures which arrived each day were a necessary but increasingly resented intrusion. Pentos was the centre of my life, but there were also other important interests; and at Pentos there were other influential figures, and power was far less concentrated than many might have thought.

There were few people in the early part of 1992 who believed that the recession, which had begun in 1990, would not finally run its course until the end of 1993. The accepted wisdom was that the recession was most likely over, but that any recovery would be anaemic; this was certainly the message which I, in common with many company chairmen, conveyed to our shareholders. The Conservative Party ran its successful election campaign in April 1992 on the theme of 'the recession is over', and 'we will reduce taxes'. Reflecting on this, and seeking to explain his failure to honour the pledge to reduce taxes (they have been significantly increased), Kenneth Clarke, the current Chancellor of the Exchequer, is quoted, in an interview in the *Spectator* on May 14, 1994, as saying, 'We seriously miscalculated the length and depth of the recession. Nobody was remotely anticipating that the recession would persist.' Our own business plans for 1992 assumed a modest and slow recovery; we were to be disappointed.

After the Conservative election victory in April, it soon became clear that the recovery was proving far more elusive than had seemed likely. Interest rates continued at a high level at a time when inflation was being reduced, so 'real' interest rates were very high indeed; the opposite of what one would have expected at this stage of the economic cycle, but membership of the exchange rate mechanism would not allow any change in policy. The ERM issue dominated economic debate in Britain in the middle months of 1992 and created great uncertainty; the eventual withdrawal from the ERM in September did not remove this uncertainty as the circumstances of withdrawal were chaotic and it was not entirely clear what the implications for future policy, not least interest rates, would be. The small signs of recovery which had seemed evident in the early months of the year had quickly been obliterated and the economy had resumed its downwards course.

Pentos's business is highly seasonal, with Christmas being the major influence. As 1992 progressed, the early feeling of hesitant optimism was replaced by the stark reality of a further deterioration in business conditions; we had taken urgent action to reduce controllable costs, particularly manning levels, although we were helpless in the face of the unremitting rise in occupancy costs; as the year drew towards its close, it was clear that we would fall seriously short of our profit objectives. On December 30, Pentos issued a 'profit warning'; this is a device for informing the stock market that its profit expectations are unlikely to be met; it helps to prevent a false market developing in the shares of the company concerned. When the final results for 1992 were published in March 1993 the full extent of the decline in profits could be seen. Although sales had increased by 15 per cent to £248 million, profit before exceptional items was only £7.5 million, compared with £15.2 million in the previous year; the main culprit responsible for the major part of the shortfall was office furniture with a loss of £300,000 against a profit of £3.7 million in 1991; interest charges were £1.5 million higher and a turnaround from profits to losses at Athena made up the rest. The story became even more dismal, as there was a charge of £3.5 million for exceptional items, mainly in respect of redundancy and reorganisation expenses, so that the profit before tax was no more than £4 million. It was the first profit reversal for twelve years; since the beginning of the 1980 recession.

In my statement which accompanied the figures, I said, 'The results of office furniture and Athena were even weaker than anticipated at the interim stage, and both businesses sustained losses. However, Dillons and Ryman again proved the quality and resilience of their businesses by increasing both sales and contribution [profit].'

Office furniture is a volatile market responding sharply to changes in the economic climate; people do not move into new offices and spend millions of pounds on systems furniture in the depths of a recession. It was, therefore, not surprising that our own office furniture business should suffer as it did; we had, unfortunately, been lulled into a false sense of security by its relatively buoyant performance in the early part of the recession, and then, mistakenly assuming that the recession was coming to an end, we were too slow to act in reducing overheads and capacity. The market was to decline further in 1993, as the recession continued, but the lower level of overhead costs meant that the losses at the Pentos office furniture business were stemmed; the market is now slowly picking up, and it should be possible gradually to rebuild its profits.

Athena is at the extreme of the spectrum both in terms of discretionary consumer spending and of operational gearing. Athena's relatively highly priced posters and prints are easy to do without when times are hard; the greetings card market tends to be more resilient, and this was reflected in Athena's own performance. A recession which bore down heavily on consumer spending was always going to hurt Athena; in addition, demographic factors were not favourable – the number of people in its youngish target market was decreasing; so Athena had fewer potential customers, and they had less money to spend. Operational gearing is the relationship between volume and profits; a business in which a small change in volume will have a large impact on profits is said to have relatively high operational gearing. Athena has far higher gross profit margins than most retailers, typically 65 per cent, and on some products much more; its prime high street position means that it also has relatively high occupancy costs, which in the short term are fixed (every five years they have leapt ahead again although the outlook is now much improved); the high gross profit on any increase in sales drops straight through to the bottom line and the converse is also true – Athena is more highly geared than almost any other retailer. Athena has battled hard against its particular vulnerability to the decline in consumer spending and its high and rising occupancy costs; it has made significant improvements in its product offer; even in its worst year, its comparable sales fell by no more than 3 per cent (which was better than many other retailers including, for example, Body Shop), and recent sales have, at last, resumed their upward trend. Athena should be a major beneficiary of economic recovery; the negative factors will become positive ones, but the high and unrealistic levels which rents have reached (despite the fact that, for some time to come, there will be no further increases) will mean that satisfactory results will not be achieved quickly.

Since the mid-Eighties we had been vigorously pursuing a programme of retail expansion; in more recent years, the onset of the recession had reduced the demand for space from other retailers, and unrepeatable opportunities had become available, particularly for the type of building from which Dillons most comfortably traded. Most of those who followed our affairs thought that this policy was far-sighted (I have described the enthusiasm and support of institutions for the Hatchards acquisition in 1990) but, as each weary year of recession was succeeded by another, there were as many who began to think it looked foolish. It depended, as always, on the time perspective; we were establishing a dominant position in markets with long-term growth prospects (the key Pentos corporate objective and its raison d'être) but in the short term it was imposing strains on our balance sheet, and, increasingly, on relationships with our shareholders; and when, in the City, it comes to a choice between short-term and long-term interests, there is just no contest. We had spent £85 million on capital projects (£100 million including acquisitions) over the previous five years, most of it on new Dillons Bookstores; we now traded from more than 500 shops, and had created almost 5000 jobs. The main source of finance had been bank borrowings which at the end of 1992 amounted to £44 million; however, in sympathy with the underlying Pentos business, cash flow was highly seasonal, and borrowings were expected to peak at around £80 million during the course of 1993; shareholders' funds were also £80 million and the level of our financial gearing, although not at the heights reached in the 1980–82 recession, had become uncomfortable. Our borrowings were clearly too high and it was important that we had a realistic plan to reduce them; we had never intended that they should reach this level, but neither had we dreamt for a moment that the recession would last so long – 1992 and now 1993 were the killers.

The poor results for 1992 and the size of the borrowings meant that we were soon again huddled together with nervous bankers. This time there were far fewer banks – we had at least learned something from the problems of the early Eighties – and the Midland and Barclays together accounted for around 90 per cent of the total facilities; it was primarily with these two banks that we discussed our business plans and our borrowing requirements during the first half of 1993. Our original trading budgets for 1993 were prepared towards the end of 1992, but before the full disappointment of the 1992 outcome was apparent; they had also been prepared in the expectation of some small improvement in the underlying economy. It was now clear that these were unrealistic, and revised budgets were prepared on more conservative assumptions. We were, at the same time, negotiating a management buy-out for the office furniture subsidiary; terms had been agreed in principle, and its management were now seeking to finalise the financing arrangements; it was hoped that we would be in a position to make an announcement with our half-year results in September. The sale of office furniture would raise a significant amount of cash, although we planned to retain a large minority interest so that we would share in any improvement in its fortunes. The level of our financial gearing would still, however, be higher than we thought prudent for the longer term. Debt levels had plagued Pentos for much of its life – not that surprising for an ambitious company starting from nothing – and I was anxious to explore every possibility in an attempt to put the level of debt finally behind us. I asked a colleague to make financial projections for the next three years on the basis of a number of different strategic options. As is usually the case with these exercises, it threw up nothing that was startlingly new, but it did help to concentrate the mind, and when his review was completed, the future suddenly seemed to possess a simple clarity. The strategic option which seemed to me to involve least risk, yet which would maximise value for shareholders, was for Pentos gradually to divest itself of all of its non-book retailing activities; this could be carried out over a period of three years on the back of what was now a realistic expectation of a slowly improving economic environment; at the completion of the exercise, Pentos would change its name to Dillons. The projections suggested that, at the end of the three-year period, we would have no debt, cash in the bank, and a respectably profitable Dillons; the business would be highly rated on the stock market, as I had no doubt that it would take to the idea of a 'pure' Dillons. It was, as in 1981, to some extent making a virtue of necessity; but, although the recession and the debt burden were acting as the catalyst, it was, perhaps, no more than accelerating a process which would eventually have unfolded. I discussed the idea with other board members, including the non-executive directors, and they shared my enthusiasm;

a formal internal paper was prepared for the board, and it was agreed that it would also be reviewed by Schroders; we hoped to be in a position to make some reference to it in the September statement. If I was not quite singing in the bath, I was certainly walking again with a spring in my step.

The talks with the Midland and Barclays, however, made slow, frustrating progress. Bankers, these days, do not cut brave figures; and there was no Stan Carslake. The meetings which I attended were deeply unimpressive, peopled by frightened, insecure executives, many of them of limited outlook, whose primary concern did not appear to be the interests of their customer. It seems as though no opportunity was lost to increase the burden of costs on Pentos and to increase the income of the banks; interest rates were raised by pushing up the bank's margin, any small change in any aspect of the facilities agreement would be used as an excuse for imposing some new ingenious facility fee, and the banks introduced a system of charging for the time their executives spent in managing the account. Teams of accountants spent weeks and months poring over our affairs, on behalf of the banks, without noticeably adding to the sum total of human knowledge, but submitting bills for hundreds of thousands of pounds and creating an enormous distraction for pressurised Pentos executives. The total additional costs in a full year, as a result of initiatives taken by the banks, probably amounted to more than two million pounds; it was not the way Stan Carslake would have done things. In 1981, when the underlying situation was much graver, we had resisted any suggestions of reporting accountants becoming involved in our affairs; Stan had accepted that it was better to allow management to focus without interruption on the task of improving financial performance;

and he had always been adamant that no bank should be allowed to exploit the strength of its position by increasing its charges and so making it that much more difficult for its customer to recover. Nonetheless, we continued to receive the support of our bankers, and there was no reason to believe that such support would not continue in the future.

As 1993 progressed, trading conditions did not improve, and as we drew close to the time for our September interim figures, it was clear that we would again fall short of external expectations for the year as a whole. For the half-year it looked as if we would be reporting a small profit or a small loss (accounting is a long way from being an exact science) and for the full year only a modest profit was anticipated. In working on the draft of the interim statement, I had written, 'Indications are that the results will be significantly below last year's level'; but I had then gone on to say, 'The influences of operational gearing from which we have suffered heavily during the recession are beginning to move in our favour. Occupancy costs are now stabilising having risen as a percentage of sales by 35 per cent over the past four years, equivalent to an additional increase in costs of £9 million.' We also hoped to include within the statement news of the proposed management buy-out of office furniture, some mention of the change in strategic direction which would focus exclusively on Dillons, and an announcement of the appointment of a chief executive which would allow me to concentrate solely on my role as chairman; so it would not all be doom and gloom. Looking a little further ahead, preliminary indications for 1994, on very conservative trading assumptions, were for an improvement in profitability to what would still be a modest and unacceptable level; but it now really did seem as if the recession was at an end and we could slowly rebuild our fortunes. We still had problems to resolve, but we were battle-hardened, and we had faced greater problems before. I had not the slightest doubt that we would be as successful in their resolution today as we had been with those of the past.

6

Not Quite the End

An informal meeting had been arranged with my non-executive directors for five o'clock on the evening of September 21, 1993.

The main purpose of the meeting was to obtain confirmation of the appointment of a new chief executive for Pentos; I was to split my roles as chairman and chief executive, which I had held since I started Pentos twenty-one years earlier, and would eventually become a part-time chairman. This was a plan I had proposed some six months earlier. It had taken longer than I had hoped to find the right candidate but I was now happy and enthusiastic about my choice. He had already been interviewed by my non-executive colleagues and the detailed terms of his employment had been agreed by them and by him, so I expected the decision to be little more than a formality. I then intended to move on to other matters, as the accumulating pressures of this never-ending recession meant that we were living in far from normal times.

Most shareholders had been sympathetic and understanding about the impact of the recession on our relatively newly established retail business. They had supported expansion and they could see the prospective virtuous circle which would exist once economic recovery eventually got under way and the operational gearing factors started to work in our favour. They were, however, unsettled from time to time by stockbrokers' analysts, who, in what seemed to be increasingly frenetic attempts to generate commission income for their employers, do not recognise shades of grey, but see every issue in dramatic tones of black and white. A tabloid prose style with appropriate headlines had often replaced painstaking academic analysis as a means of persuading institutional shareholders to 'buy' or 'sell' shares – and to hell with the company!

When our 1992 results were announced at the beginning of March 1993 I arranged to see our major shareholders on an individual basis with our finance director, Clive Gregory. In an intensive two-week period we did the rounds and saw all the important shareholders except for the largest, Mercury Asset Management (MAM), who held 15 per cent of the total equity. The response generally was supportive, with one or two exceptions; they were all, however, concerned at the relatively poor share price. The meeting with MAM had been delayed until May 6 at their request as they wanted to arrange for a number of their executives to be present and the relevant diaries had to be accommodated. MAM had expressed some dissatisfaction with the performance of Pentos, and with me in particular, in a telephone conversation with Schroders, our financial advisers, earlier in the year. The call had apparently been made by Carol Galley, a very senior fund manager at MAM, whom I had met but did not know as she did not deal with the Pentos relationship on a regular basis. At the time, I discussed the matter with my non-executive colleagues and it was felt that the appropriate response was for one of their number, Victor Blank, to speak to Carol Galley and suggest that a meeting be arranged between her and me. He made the call and she confirmed her dissatisfaction but the idea of a meeting was left in the air. So I was looking forward to the May 6 meeting as I was told that Carol Galley would be present. In the event she did not attend and we had a two-hour meeting with the fund managers who handled the shareholding on a day-to-day basis. The meeting was civil but inconclusive; they said they would see how things developed. There was little more direct feed-back from shareholders over the next few months, but the economy showed no signs of any sustained improvement and trading continued to be difficult. An early draft of the interim statement of the results for the first half of 1993 was discussed at the main board meeting held in August; it was also shown to our advisers and there was concern from one of them that the poor results would place further pressure on my own position and this message I also relayed to the non-executive directors.

From the first days of Pentos I had thought it important to have the best possible advice, particularly on legal and corporate matters, and to establish and comply with procedures which today would be called good corporate governance. This was long before the current, fashionable, Cadbury-inspired (The Cadbury Report on Corporate Governance) obsession which seeks to treat every company as if it were a mini-ICI. I have always sought to have good non-executive representation on the board. I wanted non-executives who could offer an independent objective view on issues and who could make a real contribution; I did not want establishment names who would just look good on the notepaper. At the same time I was aware of the difficulties which outsiders have in obtaining sufficient detailed knowledge of a company to be able to speak with authority; too often they will know enough to be a nuisance but not enough to be helpful. I was particularly fortunate for much of the time at Pentos to have as a non-executive colleague Philip Greer, the American businessman and venture capitalist who had been an early provider of capital for Pentos. Philip was enthusiastically committed to anything with which he was involved – there was no half-way house. His obsessions could be irritating, but he was worth his weight in gold and we became, and remain, close friends. He would devote several days to his UK board meeting visit and we spent much of that time together, so, even though he lived and worked in America, he became very knowledgeable about the Pentos businesses – and he was an important shareholder on his own and on his fund's account which made a difference. He was a director from 1973 until 1991 and he was a sad loss when, entirely because of my own stupid concern to meet perceived Cadbury and City pressure for rotation of directors, he left the board. For the past four years the board of Pentos has consisted of three non-executive directors and three executive directors under my chairmanship. Although I combined the roles of chairman and chief executive, given the balance of the board as a whole, and the stature of the non-executives, and the size of the company, we more than fully complied with the spirit of the Cadbury proposals. We have always had a de facto remuneration committee and, for example, my own pay and conditions of employment were always settled by the non-executives alone. An audit committee was established at the beginning of 1993; it consisted entirely of non-executives and it met with the finance director and the auditors without my presence or involvement. The current non-executive directors were Victor Blank, Jim Clark and Sir Kit McMahon.

Victor Blank is a fellow Mancunian although I had not known him in Manchester. I was aware of his family, particularly his uncle who was a well-known and successful, but sometimes controversial, solicitor. I met Victor shortly after I moved to London in 1969 when he was a partner in Clifford Turner (now Clifford Chance). He was an able corporate finance lawyer who had a more commercial approach to business than some of his more academic peers. He was helpful to me in the formation of Pentos in early 1972, although he could not formally act at that time because of a potential conflict of interest. We were soon, however, to be working closely together and he was involved as our corporate lawyer in all of our early dealings. In 1979 I asked him to join our board. It was unusual at Clifford Turner for partners to become directors of public companies but Victor obtained the permission of his senior partner, Raymond Clifford Turner, and Pentos became his first board appointment. We also became firm friends outside business although in recent years that friendship had waned. In 1981 Victor joined Charterhouse as head of corporate finance. It was not then common for partners of top City law firms to move into the less secure and more entrepreneurial world of merchant banking. I remember walking on Hampstead Heath with Victor as he fretfully weighed up the pros and cons. He has since made a great success at Charterhouse. Victor, therefore, had been on the board for fourteen of Pentos's twenty-one years and had been intimately involved in its affairs from the earliest days.

I recruited Jim Clark in 1977 to work as an executive in Pentos and to run a subsidiary which made prefabricated buildings. He came from the construction industry, and had worked for one of Ronnie Lyon's companies before it sank into insolvency. He had then dabbled in a small way in property development on his own account before the industry-wide banking and property problems of the time brought that to a halt. His responsibilities at Pentos soon increased to include a number of the manufacturing businesses in which Pentos was then involved until, in the early 1980s, we decided to concentrate our resources on retailing; which is when Jim's background in construction and development was invaluable. He became responsible for establishing the property development subsidiary, English and Overseas Property, on the back of our aggressive retail expansion and, in 1988 when it was floated on the Stock Exchange as a separate company, Jim was its chairman and chief executive. He had been appointed to the Pentos board as an executive director in 1980 and it was agreed, after the flotation of English and Overseas, that he would continue as a non-executive director. Jim Clark had worked for Pentos in one capacity or another for sixteen years.

I first met Kit McMahon, the third of our non-executives, sometime around 1988 when he was the chairman of Midland Bank. The Midland was one of our two main bankers and I was asked to lunch with Kit at the bank's impressive headquarters building in Poultry. He was a delightful host and the discussion over lunch was stimulating and wide-ranging and quite unlike the turgid and over-liquid affairs which were still typical of lunches with senior career executives at clearing banks. Other lunches followed and also visits to the opera and concerts. Kit McMahon was, of course, a far from typical clearing banker. He had achieved distinction as an economist before working first at the Treasury and then at the Bank of England where he became Deputy Governor. It was rumoured that he would have become Governor if he had not fallen foul of Margaret Thatcher – apparently he was not 'one of us'. He moved to the then troubled Midland Bank in 1986 and became chairman the following year. He was not perceived as a success, although I thought he was unlucky. In any event, he was unceremoniously removed in 1991. The moment I heard the news, after consulting with my colleagues, I wrote to him. I said how much I admired him and how sorry I was at what seemed to me an unfair decision. I went on to say that although Pentos was only a small company would he consider joining as a non-executive director? We had a gap to fill since Philip Greer's resignation some months earlier; and I thought that Kit, who lists 'buying books' as one of his recreations in *Who's Who*, would relate very much to the things we did and would add a new dimension at main board level. He joined the board in June 1991 and became chairman of the audit committee at the start of 1993.

We normally held six regular full board meetings each year. During the course of 1993, however, I had arranged a series of additional meetings with the non-executive directors so that they were kept more fully informed on all aspects of trading, possible disposals, banking relationships, stock market sentiment, and, not least, progress on the recruitment of a chief executive. I was, at the same time, concerned not to create a 'board within a board', which I believe is one of the potential dangers of Cadbury – another version of 'us' and 'them'. All directors have equal responsibility in law, and indeed the law does not recognise any distinction between non-executive and executive directors. In recruiting a chief executive with the aid of my non-executive colleagues I looked upon them in this context as a de facto nominations committee and I always assumed that the final candidate would need to be approved by the board as a whole, although I realised that by that stage it might be little more than a formality.

In the meetings with the non-executives I raised on several occasions my own position. I would deliberately and rather pedantically go through the options. There were four. I could continue as chairman and chief executive; or as chairman with a new chief executive; or as chief executive with a new chairman; or I could depart and we would recruit a new chairman and a new chief executive. Option two was always the preferred option, although for a very brief moment I did toy with option three. As far as the possibility that I might leave altogether was concerned it was made clear that this was an option which was just not worthy of consideration and Kit in particular was vehement on this. It was assumed that I had an important, continuing contribution to make. Nothing, therefore, had prepared me for the news I was about to hear on the evening of September 21.

The meeting was in our offices at Clifford Street in Mayfair. We had a small head office of no more than seven people. Apart from myself, there was my secretary and personal assistant, Jill Copping; Clive Gregory, the finance director; and his secretary, Brian Finch, who was the director of corporate development; and a receptionist. The boardroom is next to and connected with my own office. The three non-executives assembled there and I joined them. I took the chair and indicated that the main purpose of the meeting was to agree on a new chief executive, but that there were also other matters which we would want to discuss, and that Clive Gregory was available to join us once we had dealt with the main business. Victor Blank immediately interrupted me. He said that there was another issue which he wished to raise right at the outset, and that in saying what he was about to say he spoke for all three of the non-executive directors. They all felt, he said, that I should step down. That I should leave the company altogether. They hoped that I would remain as chairman until the year end and would then resign. The new chief executive would hopefully take up his duties within a short period of time and they would seek to appoint a new chairman by the end of the year. All of this would be announced with the interim statement which would be published within the next few days.

I was stunned. It was immediately clear to me that they were determined to remove me and that I had no ground on which to fight. No explanation for the dramatic change from our previous plans was offered. There had been some press speculation about the possible division of responsibilities and I had personally made our advisers and bankers aware of the intention to appoint a chief executive. Nobody had suggested or thought for a moment, however, that I would not be continuing as chairman. I made this point to the meeting. Victor replied by saying that the market was not yet aware of the content of the interim statement, which effectively amounted to a 'profit warning' – the second in two years. That I conceded; but, although it might well be news to the market, it was certainly not news to the non-executives and could not possibly be the reason for their volte face. I moved on to the practical problems which would need to be considered. As soon as the announcement was made my authority would disappear. I would be seen to have been publicly dismissed in humiliating circumstances. I stated that I would want to act in a way which would cause least damage to Pentos but my immediate reaction was to resign straightaway rather than wait until the end of the year. I could not see how I could continue with dignity. Nonetheless, I agreed that I would consider the matter overnight. The other issue I raised was the position of the new chief executive. All agreed that the candidate I had proposed was ideally suited for the job. I was concerned that he would be disturbed by the new arrangements. He and I had discussed with enthusiasm the prospect of working closely together and he had felt that he would need to rely on my detailed knowledge and accumulated experience for at least the next six to twelve months. It had then been assumed that I would begin to pursue a part-time role as chairman whilst remaining closely involved in book trade matters. Victor Blank said that he did not believe that there would be a problem with the candidate and he volunteered to speak to him at home that evening. I felt that there was a grave risk of having the worst of all possible worlds. If the new man were to be frightened off, then that, combined with my own dismissal, would create a power vacuum at a critical point in the fortunes of Pentos, which would be very damaging. We moved on to the remaining items on the agenda but there was no appetite on anybody's part for lengthy discussion and the meeting drifted to a desultory end. I said that I would speak to Victor the next day to let him know my decision on the timing of my departure and to hear from him of the reaction to the news from our prospective new chief executive.

It had been a traumatic meeting. I reflected, alone

in my office, on the participants. Jim Clark is a heavy, bearded, piratical-looking man in his early fifties. I have always thought that his fierce appearance belied the reality. He is quietly spoken and, in my experience, honest and straightforward in his business dealings, which in the property world cannot always be taken for granted. We had worked closely together for many years and, in 1988, I had helped him to achieve his long-held ambition to run his own public company; in 1991, I had personally helped to underwrite a rescue rights issue which had ensured its survival. At this most critical of meetings, I cannot remember that he spoke one single word. Kit McMahon is a man of wide interests, but is not a natural businessman. He is sixty-four, bespectacled and greying. He has a quizzical appearance and he had recently begun to look more than a little flustered. I might now have reservations about his judgement but I would not doubt his integrity. During the meeting, he had seemed distracted and ill-tempered. Victor Blank was clearly the leader of the pack. He is a tall, heavily built, lugubrious, large-featured man of fifty-two. He had secured his financial independence as a result of his participation in the Woolworth's buy-out which he had helped to organise whilst at Charterhouse. He has an easy charm which he has used to good effect. Beneath the cheerful and easy-going exterior, however, is a hard, steely centre. Victor knows what he wants and he usually gets it. We had been friends and colleagues for more than twenty years but he spoke to me in a direct and almost brutal manner. When the chips are down there are no soft words or platitudes from Victor; and it was he who had done most of the talking. Kit might have helped to load the gun, but it was Victor who had pulled the trigger.

My own position was impossible. There was nothing

I could do against the combined might of the three non-executives. I tried to let this sink in. There had been mistakes in recent years and the recession had been relentless and unforgiving. But the mistakes had mainly been matters of judgement on the length and depth of the recession; with the benefit of hindsight we would not have continued to expand at such a rate if we had thought that the recovery was to be so long delayed. We were not the only people to have misjudged the economy. And the policies which we had pursued at Pentos had been agreed by the board as a whole. Those policies had achieved considerable success in earlier years and Dillons, Athena and Ryman had been established as major retail brands. Clearly, I was responsible for the problems which Pentos now faced; but I was convinced that the plans I had put forward for a new strategic direction, a reduction in borrowings, and the appointment of a new chief executive and my continuance as chairman, were the best and safest way forward, and eventually the economy would recover. I had said many times over the years to my friends, when facing other problems, and fighting through other recessions, that the important thing in business is to keep your place at the table. When the cards are reshuffled and redealt you must still be there to have a chance of recouping your losses. I had faced many difficulties in the past but I had always been able to keep to that rule; now my chair had been kicked away from under me.

The following morning, Wednesday, September 22, I had separate meetings with Jill Copping, my secretary; Frank Brazier, the main board director responsible for Dillons; and Clive Gregory, the finance director. Jill had worked with me for six years and was loyal, hard-working and dedicated to Pentos; she ran the corporate head office and was invariably the first to arrive each morning. I brought Frank into Pentos in 1983; he had been responsible for the dramatic development of the Dillons chain and for its success; book sales under his leadership had increased from less than £10 million to £150 million and Dillons was now the UK's largest specialist book retailer; he had been appointed to the main board in 1986. Clive had first worked for Pentos in 1975 in its very early days; he had then led a management buy-out of the Halls greenhouse business, but had returned at my request as finance director, just twelve months earlier. The separate meetings were brief and emotional with the news being accepted with incomprehension and helpless resignation. The response from the third executive director, Brian Matthews, was a little different. Brian had joined Pentos in 1981; from small beginnings he had built our office furniture manufacturing subsidiary into the second largest in the UK. He was now with my encouragement seeking to fund a management buy-out. I spoke with him on the telephone at the factory in Derbyshire; his response was angry and he said 'they' must not get away with it, and what can be done? I persuaded him that nothing could be done; that I believed the actions of the non-executives were not meant to be vindictive but reflected the prevalent culture in the City. They wanted to be seen to be acting in the right way – whatever current practice or fashion dictated that to be; it was backside-covering time. The question was – who would look after the business?

I left my office to get some fresh air. I felt emotionally drained and very confused. I walked to Hatchards in Piccadilly but quickly had to leave the shop. This was not going to be easy; and the impossibility of continuing for three more months was already becoming clear.

A previously-arranged meeting was held in my offices with Schroders, Norton Rose, our solicitors, and Pentos executives later in the day. It was to discuss some of the issues to be included in the impending interim statement. I had added a new paragraph to the draft statement on the management changes and I had shown this to Linda Collier, the Schroders director newly responsible for Pentos, privately, just before the meeting so she was not caught unawares. Schroders emphasised the need to present the news in a positive way; we must focus on the new chief executive and look forward to the future rather than dwelling on the past. It was, therefore, absolutely critical that the new chief executive was on board. Victor Blank had, as promised, spoken to the candidate the previous evening and Victor had reported to me that he did not foresee any problems, but that he, the candidate, would be speaking to his present employer at the end of the week, and final clearance and a starting date were expected at the beginning of the following week. It was very tight. We had decided that we could not delay the interim statement much longer and therefore had fixed on Wednesday, September 29 as the announcement day. Schroders thought it might be helpful to use a financial public relations company to deal with the press and to try to get the positive, forward-looking emphasis on the news which we wanted. They were aware of my deep cynicism so far as public relations consultants were concerned, particularly financial public relations. I had never been convinced that people who at best half-understood your business could do a better job of discussing it with the press and the City than the executives whose daily life it was; and too often the principals of a PR company would make a reasonably impressive presentation in pitching for a new assignment and you would then find that the day-to-day handling of the account was in the hands of some inexperienced junior executive who knew absolutely nothing. However, in these unusual circumstances and with what would be a narrowly defined brief, I allowed myself to be persuaded.

I met Lucas Van Praag of Brunswick PR and Alan Jacobs of Schroders two days later on the Friday morning in my office. Brian Finch also joined us. Lucas was clearly rattled to hear that we did not yet have final confirmation on the new chief executive. Without him, it would be a very different story; one of unalloyed gloom. The market would hardly be reassured to be told of my departure but with no named successor. In fact Lucas asked to speak to me privately after the meeting and told me that I could not possibly announce my resignation as both chairman and chief executive if a new chief executive was not immediately available. I said that I had been given no alternative. The other issue which Lucas raised was his concern that none of this news should leak into the weekend press. There had in recent months been a number of speculative stories in the Sunday newspapers which had been unsettling. They were mainly inaccurate but nonetheless there had been elements which had suggested some insider knowledge. We checked through the very small list of people who were aware of the new paragraph on management changes which was now part of the draft interim statement and determined to be doubly vigilant.

The next day I was at home, in the country, at Saturday lunch when the telephone rang. It was John Jay, the City editor of the *Sunday Telegraph*. I knew John well and had first met him some ten years ago when he started as a City journalist. Our worst fears were confirmed. He told me that he understood that I was going to resign, that it would be announced next week, and that he was going to run the story in his paper tomorrow. Did I have any comment? I sought to make light of it. I said that there had been speculation for some time about my position and that it was hardly a new story. He replied very firmly that this was a new story because he had been informed that there would be a statement next week; that it would announce a new chief executive; and that I was to resign as chairman and from the board at the end of the year; I was being ousted by the non-executives. I said that he would not expect me to comment and I couldn't. The following day the story appeared on the front page of the business section of the *Sunday Telegraph*. It had every detail and it was correct in every detail. He had very good information.

We conducted a post-mortem on the story with Brunswick and with Schroders on the Monday morning. Brunswick's findings were that there had been a deliberate leak with the intention, as they put it, of 'cutting the legs from under me' – making it impossible for me to defend my position. I did not realise I still had a position to defend. It was a pointless act which caused great unrest within the company and which added to my public humiliation; it made an already intolerable situation that much more difficult. It was also to have repercussions.

I had convened a meeting of the full board for the Tuesday morning to approve the final form of the interim statement, including the paragraph dealing with the management changes. These had not yet been considered by the board as a whole, however much of a formality that might be. Of course, the key unresolved issue was the position of the new chief executive. I was still waiting to get his final confirmation, and to agree his starting date. Having his name in the slot was crucial to the statement.

The headhunter we were using kept reassuring me that there was no cause for concern. I was told to expect a telephone call on the Monday evening or first thing on Tuesday morning before the board meeting. The call eventually came through at half past eight on the Tuesday morning. It was bad news. He had decided not to make the move. He said that three factors had changed his mind. First, he had had an encouraging discussion about his future prospects at his present company. It was, however, the other two factors which he said had been crucial. He was very unhappy at the fact that I would not be working with him and he, and as importantly his wife, had been disturbed by the weekend press comment. He was not going to change his mind. I gave the bleak news to the rest of the board.

The board meeting did not last long. Each of the key issues included in the interim statement was carefully considered. Clive Gregory gave an update on the likely out-turn for the year as a whole. Kit McMahon, quite properly, was anxious that the comments made in the statement on prospects were, on conservative assumptions, consistent with our current profit expectations. He declared himself satisfied; as did the rest of the board. I haltingly read the paragraph on management changes, which was received in total silence. I then moved on more quickly and easily to a practical point. I suggested that, to aid communication and continuity until a new chief executive could be recruited and appointed, those executives who had hitherto reported directly to me should now report to Clive Gregory and that he, in turn, would report to Kit and myself jointly until my departure – I had decided to resign at the end of October – and to Kit solely thereafter. This was agreed, although it was later misinterpreted by Clive, I am sure innocently, that the decision had been for him to report to Kit solely, with immediate effect.

The announcement was made to the Stock Exchange on Wednesday morning at eleven o'clock.

I was in the office the following day, but then left for a week's holiday in Switzerland. Amongst the calls which I took before I left was one from Philip Greer who was telephoning from New York. He had seen the news on the front page of that day's *Financial Times*. He simply said, 'Terry, I don't know the background to all this but I can tell you one thing. If I had been there it would not have happened.'

I did not see any newspapers whilst I was away, which for me was, to say the least, unusual. After Thursday's press, there were apparently a number of follow-up stories in the Sunday papers. In one, I am told, it was reported that I had departed as a result of an institutional shareholder coup masterminded by Carol Galley of MAM. If that was the case it was certainly unknown to me, although I now understand that the non-executive directors did have a meeting with MAM, but that it was after the events I have described above.

I returned to my office after the holiday. It was October 11. Still three weeks to get through. When I walked into Clive Gregory's office he looked at me as if at a ghost – Lazarus raised from the dead. He said that he was surprised to see me and that he had thought I would have stayed at home. It was clear that, in my absence, things had already moved on. A board meeting had been held of which I had been unaware and of which I had not received notice. Clive, a mountain of a man who weighed more than twenty stone, seemed sheepish and ill at ease and was later to be extremely emotional at what he thought were the enormous pressures under which he was being placed. It seemed that the profit expectations about which Clive had been so confident just a week before were already being downgraded, although I saw no figures or papers; indeed, I was to see no more board papers subsequent to the meeting of September 28. Clive explained in some embarrassment that he was preparing a 'kitchen sink' job – a colourful stock market description of the wide-scale accounting provisions which a new management typically makes to place conveniently on the doorstep of its predecessor. Victor Blank, he said, had asked him to leave no stone unturned in his search for items which could be added to the list.

I made several half-hearted attempts to re-engage in these last few days but to no avail. The final day could not arrive quickly enough. It at last arrived – Friday, October 29. I had arranged to take those who worked closely with me out to lunch. Joe, my chauffeur for many years, then drove me for the last time on the two-hour journey from Mayfair to Whichford, our home in the Cotswolds. Although I had been avoiding newspapers, Jill had given one press cutting to me from the *Sunday Times* which she thought I would like to see. It was a comment written by Ivan Fallon, whom I had known throughout my business career. In it he remembered the 'big dream' I had for Pentos right from the start. It had taken twenty-one years to build; and in just four weeks it had been destroyed.

There was, however, one last scene of farce still to be played. During my final three weeks I had tried to keep in touch with progress on the resumed search for a chief executive. The headhunter had helpfully kept me informed without mentioning names of potential candidates. The assignment was of course being handled entirely by the non-executives. Progress had been more rapid than might have been expected, partly, as it turned out, because the front runner had been a candidate in the earlier search. It was hoped an announcement would be made to coincide with my physical departure. In the event it was slightly delayed and a statement was issued on the afternoon of Thursday, November 4 with the news of the name of the new chief executive, who was to take up his duties on January 1, of Kit McMahon's appointment as chairman, and of my formal resignation from the board. There had been no board meeting; the executive directors had not met the new chief executive, and Frank Brazier was aware of his name only from the draft press release which he saw on the day of its issue; as the board had not met, Kit McMahon could not have been elected chairman; and the public could read the news at lunchtime in that day's *Evening Standard* before the statement was formally lodged with the Stock Exchange. The habit of leaking was clearly proving difficult to break.

Throughout this period, the non-executive directors had acted as if they were the board; as if they alone bore the responsibility for the company. They created great instability, which still persists, at a delicate time in Pentos's fortunes. They were motivated by the desire to follow what they believed to be the spirit of the Cadbury proposals; to be seen to be doing what current City fashion would judge to be the 'right thing'; which is not quite the same as acting in the best long-term interests of the company and its shareholders.

It was not meant to end like that; and it need not have done. Two months later, John Osborne was writing in the *Spectator* after the 'public desecration' of *The Entertainer* by the BBC: 'It's only a play you may say. It will pass and is already forgotten. Yet it is my life, my limbs that have been severed.'

7

Reflections

The promised 'kitchen sink' job duly arrived; and it was the mother and father of 'kitchen sink' jobs. The same non-executive directors, the same finance director, and the same auditors were able, following the same accounting policies, to convert the small profit envisaged at the September board meeting into a total loss of £70 million; admittedly, £14 million of this was simply a transfer from one line on the balance sheet to another, but the rest consisted of a wide range of provisions including provisions for losses on disposals, exceptional items and apparent trading losses of mammoth proportions. These appalling results were accompanied by a rights issue to raise £45 million at 25p per share. This was not the way we had done things in 1981, and it is not what I would have done now. In 1981, we did not have the luxury of being able to write off or provide for almost every asset in the balance sheet and then have the opportunity of presiding over a seemingly miraculous recovery; we had a three-year slog to get the business and the balance sheet in shape and then had a rights issue from a position of strength. In 1994, my approach would have been the same; to reduce debt by the disposal, over a three-year period, of all of the newly defined peripheral businesses, and to concentrate resources on Dillons. A rights issue would then most likely not have been required, but, if it had, it would have been launched from a firmer base, which would have been very much better for shareholders.

The media took the figures without even the tiniest grain of salt, when, perhaps, a lorry-load was necessary. Some newspapers wrote the story as if I were a recently hired hand who had been found with his fingers in the till, and the many years of success were ignored. Stockbrokers' analysts also suspended disbelief, and, having previously only smelt blood, they now feasted on it (by no means all of the retail analysts had become negative, however, one of the most perceptive, and as it turned out also most prescient, having written to me in October to say, 'It is perhaps inevitable that whoever fills your shoes at Pentos will seek to rewrite history, however I believe in Dillons you have created a major retail brand at a time when most businesses were heading in the opposite direction and this will always be recognised as your greatest achievement'). The gross income from reverse premiums had been disclosed for the first time (although the accounting policy was not changed) and my earlier fears about the naive, simplistic and misleading way in which this information would be used were fully justified; the other side of the equation, the start-up costs, were entirely ignored, and it was assumed that reported profits should be reduced by the gross amount of the reverse premiums; no wonder no other retailer had wanted to run this particular gauntlet.

At the beginning of November, I had received a letter

from Kit McMahon in which he generously wrote of his 'enormous admiration for what you have done at Pentos'; on Dillons he added, 'Yours has been a major creative achievement. The concept is widely recognised to have been brilliant and there is absolutely no doubt that the brand and the shops will go from strength in the years ahead – once we finally emerge from this wretched recession which has in the short term dealt such cruel blows to your plans.' On the events of the previous September, however, he threw no further light. 'Things had got to a point,' he wrote, 'when what happened had to happen – and there is perhaps no point in jobbing back over the details.' He mentioned the name of the new chief executive – news which he rightly judged I would receive with 'unease'. I have heard nothing further from any of my former non-executive colleagues. In the 1993 Annual Report, Kit McMahon, in his first statement as chairman, paid fulsome tribute to Victor Blank's contribution to the company over fifteen years, and wrote warmly of Clive Gregory's two-year stint. There was no reference to me; my name was not mentioned; as in a Soviet purge, I had become a non-person. An *Evening Standard* journalist calling the Pentos head office for my telephone number was told to look in the directory.

There have been other changes. Some of my long-standing and trusted colleagues, including Frank Brazier who did so much to help build the Dillons chain, have been asked to leave; other experienced managers have also left, and, at Dillons, many essential texts are missing from the shelves, and the general appearance of those shops which I have visited has sharply deteriorated. The feeling of unease has grown. Consultants, whom I would rarely let inside the door, now proliferate; I am told that they call the shots, but fervently hope that this is not the case, as there is nothing more dangerous than those who peddle their instant remedies without the checks and challenges of sceptical, seasoned and experienced managers. There have already been changes, in part of emphasis, but also more widely, in the trading policies and market positioning of the three retail chains. Those mooted, and partially implemented, at Athena and Ryman involve risks which would worry me, but my major concern is at Dillons. Dillons' success is based on the unrivalled reputation it has established for range and service; both of these are now being undermined, with a deliberate move to a stock policy which concentrates on a narrower range of best-selling titles and an approach to manning levels which places less reliance on experienced and knowledgeable staff; these changes will destroy Dillons' competitive advantage and make it little different from W.H. Smith. I hope that as new management becomes more experienced it will quickly come to realise what a very special business it has inherited at Dillons and that there is no need to attempt to re-invent the wheel.

There is no reason why Pentos should not prosper. It has survived three recessions, and this most damaging of recessions is now at an end; it has (despite my reservations on terms and timing) the cash from the rights issue; most importantly it has three of Britain's best-known retail brands, and, in Dillons, possibly the world's best book chain. Its success will depend totally on its ability to protect and develop further the reputation and integrity of those brands, as reputations which have taken years to become established can be lost overnight. A large part of my life was given to Pentos, and much of Pentos is in me. It often seemed that we were indivisible, and it is sometimes difficult for me to accept that I will not now preside over its recovery, particularly as I pass a shop window or spot a familiar shopping bag in the streets. It is a better company than some current fashionable comment portrays, and it deserves a better and more tranquil future. I will be watching with more than a passing interest.

As I re-read this story and reflect on my experiences, there are certain issues which recur, and others which have assumed a prominence only recently. Overall, it is by no means obvious to me that the business environment has improved during the past twenty years. The banks continue to be poorly managed; the sheer scale of the economic incompetence of successive governments beggars belief; stockbrokers' analysts have grown massively in numbers and influence but this has not been matched in quality; the financial press continue to trivialise and personalise business and City issues; auditors have sprouted numerous new tentacles which pose serious questions of conflict of interest; the new obsession with corporate governance is divisive and has created a uniform and uncomfortable strait-jacket for all companies which favours form over content; the increasing power of the fund managers and their myopic attitudes are a threat to business enterprise and development; and it is the financial ideas and deals which have made the money rather than the provision of goods and services.

To start with the last point first: it is difficult, in Britain, to make serious money in the real world of making 'things' which people want and in providing services which they need; it is easier to make money in the world of deals, and financial innovation and financial engineering – widgets have lost out to paper. It applies to individuals as well as to companies. Successful merchant bankers and stockbrokers make the kind of money which managers in industry can only dream about; there are now one or two exceptions in industry, but they are people at the top of large companies – in the City, middle-ranking executives can earn telephone number salaries; it is not surprising that ambitious men and women are drawn to the City rather than to industry. As far as companies are concerned, it takes time to develop a product, break into a market and establish a profitable business. It helps if there is a stable economic environment and patient long-term investors, and that has not always been the case in recent years. The City has preferred the easier pickings of the financial markets fed on its staple diet of bids and deals. The City likes deals; it makes its money from them and they often provide the short-term performance surge which the fund managers crave. Even within the book trade it was Paul Hamlyn's dealing abilities as much as his business-building skills which made him his fortune; and Tim Waterstone seized a unique opportunity to convert his then rather indifferent business into a large amount of money. In my own modest financial affairs, there have been three things which have been important: the original deal in 1972 in which Pentos reversed into the Cape Town and District Gas Light and Coke Company Limited, and obtained its stock market quotation; the innovative deferred shares capitalisation issue of 1979; and my pension arrangements, which, although conventional, are an essential source of security. The serious business of building a worthwhile company over twenty years on which I have concentrated all my energies has been of little personal financial benefit. The Pentos share price started at the equivalent of 5p in 1972, reached 103p in 1979, subsided to 6p in the final year of the 1980–82 recession, and reached its all-time high of 184p in the summer of 1987 before the stock market crash of Black Monday. It had recovered again to 171p in 1991, but by October 1993 (the final year of the 1990–93 recession) when I left, it had fallen to 43p; I still owned the same number of shares as I had at the outset in 1972 (my percentage shareholding had, however, declined from 29 per cent to 2 per cent due to the new shares that had been issued over the years to fund expansion, although I remained by far the largest personal shareholder and always had more at risk than any other individual). Long-term investors in Pentos had invariably done well and I have no doubt that, given time, Pentos's fortunes and share price would again have revived and would have established new records. I had not, however, realised that I was already so close to the finishing post.

Although the banks have not become more efficient, they have certainly become more greedy; and this is not up-front, straightforward honest greed, but, like a robber lurking in an alley-way waiting to pounce on an old lady feeling her way home in the dark, they catch you when you are at your most vulnerable. This marks a distinct change over the past ten to fifteen years. In the days of Stan Carslake, a company seeking the indulgence of its bankers whilst problems were resolved would receive a more constructive response than would be likely today. The price of support has been jacked up in an unconscionable manner and it makes eventual recovery a more difficult prospect. Bankers are less secure than before, and the state of indecisive demoralised fear which recently existed in at least one of the major clearing banks was almost tangible; they do not seem happy at their work. However, some of the proven old-fashioned values still apply: long-standing open relationships (with regular contact being maintained at several levels) with just a small number of banks is the most likely way to keep out of trouble. (Pentos had banked with both Barclays and the Midland since 1972.) Companies which borrow from a large number of different banks are those more likely to have difficulties in obtaining support; lenders with a relatively small amount at risk, and with whom at best there is only a tenuous relationship, will look to cut and run at the first hint of trouble, and this can destabilise the whole structure of banking arrangements. And, of course, it continues to hold true that the more you owe a bank the less likely it is to take precipitate action.

It is a mistake to expect much of any government, but even those of us with the lowest of expectations have been bitterly disappointed by the inept performance, particularly in economic matters, of recent administrations. My concerns are mainly in areas in which government policy most obviously affects new business development: a more stable environment in which businessmen can plan with greater confidence, open and free conditions in competitive markets, and a tax policy which does not distort investment flows. There is now more than enough evidence, in this country and elsewhere, to prove beyond the slightest doubt that, if we are going to achieve sustained economic growth and a reduction in unemployment, then it can only be on the back of new business formation; put very simply, it is small companies which create new jobs not large ones. An even and consistent economic policy is the most important prerequisite for creating the conditions in which new enterprises will be launched with a better than even chance of survival. Most entrepreneurs in the past twenty years have been brought down by the boom and bust philosophy of successive governments seeking electoral advantage; it is instructive to note that of my own peers from the class of 1972 hardly any have survived. The cost in financial and human terms of weak, uncertain and, at times, vainglorious government cannot be overstated. A new bill on competition policy has been promised since 1989; it is long, long overdue. We need strong legislation to deal with restrictive practices and the abuse of market power. There are two issues, both of which are particularly relevant to small businesses, which I would then like to see reviewed against assumed tougher criteria (in addition, obviously, to the net book agreement): the competitive forces (or lack of them) within the commercial banking system, and institutional property leases and the landlord/tenant relationship. I would also like to see the Office of Fair Trading and the Monopolies and Mergers Commission made fully independent of government; a move made more urgent as a result of the reported increased influence and involvement in their affairs of the President of the Board of Trade. Savings and investment funds in Britain are mainly directed towards home ownership and retirement pensions provision because of the distorting effect of their favourable tax treatment. The trade-off is that tax rates are higher than would be the case without these concessions, and that it limits the funds which would otherwise be available for other forms of investment. Tax relief on home ownership, although still enormous in terms of cost to the Exchequer (around £4 billion per annum), has recently been reduced and there is now a wider understanding of some of the risks involved in buying a house (certainly a highly geared purchase) as well as the benefits. Tax relief on pensions is in three parts: contributions to pension funds by the individual are allowable against earnings, the contributions of the employer are allowable against profits, and the income of pension funds is effectively free of both income tax and capital gains tax; the cost of these incentives (more than £10 billion each year) now far outweighs that for home ownership, and it is growing rapidly. I would like to see a move towards tax neutrality and the abolition, over a number of years, of all tax allowances which artificially distort investment decisions; it could mean a reduction of 8p in the basic rate of income tax, but of equal importance is the fact that savings and investment patterns would become more varied. Direct investment, as the effective discrimination against it is removed, would, for example, become at least as attractive (as it is in the United States and other countries) as pension fund investment; I believe, as I will explain, that the concentration of resources and power in pension fund management is unhealthy and is inimical to the interests of much of British industry and certainly of small businesses which are starved of investment.

The growth in the number and influence of analysts has been matched only by that of financial public relations consultants; each has a direct line to his or her currently favoured journalist in the financial press. There are some excellent journalists who write on the City and on business – Ivan Fallon (despite the increasingly tabloid approach of the *Sunday Times Business News*), Neil Collins, John Jay, Christopher Fildes, Ray Snoddy and Robert Peston spring to mind, and the list is by no means exhaustive. Most financial journalists, however, and much of the media (including television) do not encourage a wider understanding of business and City affairs, and this is important, as it allows the myth of the City as a casino to be perpetuated in influential areas of politics and government and it also results in too many people equating the City with business. Much of what is written is superficial (often little more than the company press handout); original comment is often sensationalised or concerned with trivial or personalised issues; and a major part of many City pages looks like a rather poor-quality stock market tip sheet. It is a truism to state that the first thing any financial journalist does when receiving a company's annual report is to look up the chairman's salary; board remuneration is an important issue, but the need to pursue relentlessly the currently fashionable cause has meant a loss of any kind of perspective, and much more important matters are often overlooked. The cult of personality now pervades every area of public life, and business is no exception; reputations are built up with uncritical adulation and then mercilessly destroyed without the reader ever being made aware that business is, after all, a fairly serious, complex and important activity. Increasingly, however, it is not a businessman whose name appears in a City story, but a public relations prima donna or a 'star' analyst; and these are the informers who are providing the 'news' and influencing its presentation. Analysts and public relations consultants are now too often concerned with their own self-promotion and they get between the company and the businessman on the one side and shareholders and the wider outside world on the other. My own approach has always been to take or return calls from the press and to establish personal direct links with major shareholders. It is important to maintain this open relationship of availability through good and bad times, and in the long run – despite my own recent personal experiences – I believe it to be the best policy; communications is an essential part of a chairman's job and is far too important to be left to others.

The major accounting firms are now large-scale, international, financial conglomerates. They are involved in every area of corporate activity; literally from a company's birth to its death. They offer advisory services on company formations, flotations, acquisitions and disposals, management consultancy, management recruitment, information technology and taxation; they are involved in the corporate knacker's yard of receivership and administration and they offer a wide range of other services; and, I almost forgot, they also act as auditors. In many areas they are now competing with merchant banks and other specialists, but whereas a company does not need to have a merchant bank the law insists that it has an auditor. Auditors have used the close and privileged relationship which they inevitably enjoy with their clients as a result of their statutory position, to market their other services – and with devastating success. The top six accounting firms are now bigger than all but their very largest clients; because not only does every company have to have an auditor, but, if it is to enjoy the best credit-rating and the highest stock market basis of valuation, then its accounts must be audited by one of the top firms. As audit work becomes concentrated on the top six they then compete aggressively with each other, using the audit fee as a loss leader; because, once the foot is in the door, the pickings can be enormous and the audit fee will usually be only a small proportion of the total income which can be earned from the audit client. Once established, an auditor will be anxious to maintain his position so that he can continue to enjoy his financial bonanza; it would be surprising if there were not occasions when this consideration did not affect his judgement. Accounting conventions, despite much work by the accounting bodies, are not always capable of precise definition and allow too much scope for presentation; there is all too often the need to rely on personal judgement. It is not exaggerating to state that, if one took as an example a typical, acquisition-led, international conglomerate with reported profits of say £100 million, then the same facts could as easily be converted to a loss of £100 million, and vice versa. The clear, unambiguous independence of auditors should be paramount. It is impossible for investors to have sufficient confidence in accounts whilst the present regime exists. A review of the auditing profession is long overdue, but I would make one very simple change: an auditor should not be allowed to provide any other services to or derive any other pecuniary advantage from his audit client.

If the traditional role of the auditor was re-established, and his independence from management and responsibility to shareholders strengthened, then there would be less need to implement the enterprise-stifling proposals of the Cadbury Report on corporate governance. Cadbury taken as a whole is a depressing and negative document which seeks to create a single set of rules to be applied to each individual company regardless of size or the nature of its business; it is a knee-jerk reaction to a number of headline-making corporate failures which although spectacular have been relatively rare. There are some obvious and sensible proposals within it (many of which had been implemented at Pentos long before Cadbury had been thought of, although I must own up to having introduced changes more recently for their cosmetic appeal to the City rather than for their practical value); the overall effect, however, is to emphasise the fear of failure (another form of the British disease) and to give a low priority to wealth-creating innovation; and, without my wanting to appear too cynical, it is difficult to see that audit committees have yet improved confidence in accounts, or that remuneration committees have even slightly dented the real corporate obscenity of boardroom pay. Cadbury also deals a devastating blow to the concept of the unitary board and creates a real division between non-executive directors and executive directors, with the executives definitely coming off second best. In the events which I have described at Pentos in 1993, the non- executives acted as if they were the board and totally ignored the executives, who were left in a state of confused apprehension; that cannot be the right way to do things.

The development over the past two decades which has caused me the greatest unease, however, more than the incompetence of government, the acquiescence of auditors or the rapacity of banks, has been the growing dominance of the financial institutions and their obsessive, homogeneous short-termism. Individuals today own only 20 per cent of company shares compared to 50 per cent thirty years ago; in the United States 50 per cent are still held directly by individuals. By far the most important and fastest-growing single source of stock market investment is now represented by the pension funds, and that is my main area of concern; they account for 35 per cent of total UK equities compared to only 7 per cent thirty years ago, and in that time, pension fund assets under management have increased in money terms by a factor of one hundred and in relative terms by a factor of ten (PDFM research). As individuals tend to remain loyal to the companies in which they invest and to retain their shareholdings for longer than average periods of time, and as pension funds are at the other end of the spectrum, this dramatic change in share ownership (encouraged by our fiscal system) has created greater volatility in share prices and has undermined the stability of many companies.

The average holding period for UK equities in pension fund portfolios was 15 years in the 1960s, 6 years in the 1970s and 5 years in the 1980s (PDFM Research), proof enough of the increasing short-termism of pension fund investment; and as these figures are average figures and blue-chip investments which represent 'core' holdings will be held for longer periods of time, this suggests a much higher activity rate for smaller companies.

Pension fund management is enormously lucrative, fiercely competitive, and, just as with the accounting firms, power is now concentrated in very few hands. Ironically, the post-Maxwell climate bears some responsibility for this, as pension fund trustees play safe by insisting on a top, blue-chip name as fund manager. The net effect is that just four management companies were running funds which accounted for 27 per cent of the occupational scheme total at the end of 1993; as many of the biggest funds are run in-house, this probably represented between 40 per cent and 50 per cent of the free market. The four companies were Mercury Asset Management (MAM), Philips and Drew (PDFM), Schroder Investment Management, and BZW Investment Management, and between them they controlled funds of £115 billion, up 37 per cent in just one year; MAM is the largest and has the reputation of being the most aggresive, and it alone was responsible for £41 billion. It would not be an exaggeration to say that those four companies are probably the most powerful in the City. The way in which pension fund performance is measured, and the intensely competitive environment, make the obsession with the short term inevitable. Pension funds' market investments are valued, literally, every day, and the fund managers will appear before the trustees for the quarterly meeting with comparative performance tables; if the fund fails to match the *Financial Times* index, or performs less well than the average fund, or, heaven forbid, is placed in the lower quartile, then questions will be asked; and, if the underperformance continues, then new managers will be appointed. (The irony is that actuaries who report on whether a pension fund has sufficient assets to meet its future liabilities quite properly take a long-term view, looking as far as twenty-five years ahead; in valuing the investments of the fund, they will usually ignore the share prices of a particular day, and instead assess the value of the anticipated future income flow from those investments.) The pressure to perform day in, day out, quarter after quarter, is relentless; at one institutional lunch, the fund manager complained petulantly that I (she meant the Pentos share price) was responsible for a negative 0.7 per cent in her performance charts in the previous quarter, and it was quite clear that nothing else was quite as important as that. Against this background it would take a brave fund manager to step out of line; short-termism and me-toism pervade and the avoidance of risk is paramount. This in turn breeds a new type of industrial manager who will also have risk avoidance as his guiding principle; the last thing he will wish to do will be to disappoint or 'surprise' his all-powerful pension fund shareholders; and, again following the example of pension fund shareholders who have no commitment to a company, but shuffle their short-term investments at the whim of the moment, so executives have become more footloose and less committed and are more likely to move on to their next company when the share options are cashed and before their mistakes are found out. More than one can play the short-term game. But this is not good for wealth creation, it is not good for small businesses which are starved of much-needed capital, and it is not good for Britain. What can be done? There are no easy solutions, but the first thing to do, as I have already suggested, is to take away the tax privileges of pension funds so that resources are freed for a wider range of savings and investment media. Apart from that one crucially important act of removing an existing distortion, I am not sure that government action is the answer. There has to be an exercise in enlightened self-interest; the higher echelons of the City have got to be convinced that longer-term policies will pay better longer-term dividends. We need the equivalent of a Warren Buffet, who became the second richest American from pursuing a policy of significant, committed, long-term investment in a relatively small number of companies; the exact opposite of the policy followed by the typical UK fund manager. The City should act now to put its own house in order; it should give the same high-profile priority to an in-depth report on investment policy and short-termism as it did to corporate governance; and it is a much worthier cause. Any initiative would certainly receive the support of the main political parties; and, as short-termism is back on the political agenda, it might pre-empt action from some future government which would be unwelcome and almost certainly counter-productive. There has got to be a better way.

That is really the end of this story. Much has happened since I left Manchester for London in 1969; and I have travelled further than I could ever have imagined from the mean streets of inner city life in the late 1930s. I am proud of what has been created at Pentos, but I could and should have achieved far more, and any disappointment which I feel is not just for myself but for my family, friends, supporters and colleagues, all of whom deserved better. I have no complaints; I have had my chances, even if I have not always taken full advantage of them. But what I have done I have always done with enthusiasm, with commitment and with conviction; I have also – and this has been a fatal mistake in the eyes of some people – allowed myself to become emotionally involved in my business. I would have had it no other way.

Postscript

At 9.00 a.m. on March 1, 1995, I heard the heart-stopping news that administrative receivers had been appointed to Pentos. It seemed that the £45 million raised from shareholders only nine months earlier was gone, and that the banks' patience had finally run out.

I have earlier attempted to set out frankly the problems which Pentos faced in 1993. Most were the result of the prolonged recession and rapidly increased rental costs. However, the recession had ended, rent escalation had disappeared, and, given time, all of the problems were capable of resolution. The cash from the rights issue should have been a bonus. So what went wrong?

I had, in writing the hardback edition of this book, set out fairly gently some of my reservations and concerns about the new trading policies which had then recently been introduced. I had, at the same time, expressed the hope – and it was also my belief – that these policies would be changed as a better understanding of the businesses was developed. Unfortunately, this did not happen.

At Dillons, the new emphasis on stock-turn was continued and stock levels were reduced by an absolute ban on buying new books from publishers and by a massive 'clearance' sale. By a bizarre act of misplanning, a massive £1.5 million media advertising programme was run in parallel with the stock-buying ban – promoting books which were not on the shelves. Dillons' reputation and authority – its enormous success – were based upon its wide range of stock and its experienced and knowledgeable staff. It was not surprising, therefore, that sales in the shops, despite the advertising campaign, were quickly running at more than a 25% reduction on the previous year, and this eventually led to a partial reversal of the new stockholding policy. But the damage had been done. It takes much longer to rebuild specialist stocks than to run them down; the choice of books in the shops never fully recovered.

At Ryman, the story can best be told by quoting from a letter which Roy Crosland (Ryman's former, and successful, managing director) had published in the *Financial Times*:

> The real reason for an astonishing loss of nearly £5 million in 1994 was the decision by the new management, egged on by the consultants, analysts and others, to reduce prices in the mistaken belief this would counter a non-existent switch to out-of-town competitors and boost volumes. This destroyed margins without having any effect on sales and showed a fundamental misunderstanding of the business. Ryman is, and always has been, a convenience store for small purchases. No one buys bulk stationery supplies from it. The average purchase is £5 and, within reason, demand is price-inelastic. Store location, service levels and availability are the issues, not price. Ryman is fundamentally a sound business competing in a different market from out-of-town operators.

The Athena business faced special difficulties. Its produces were highly discretionary (easy to do without when times are hard) and its target market had suffered from adverse demographic factors (there were fewer people in its youngish age group). Nonetheless, its customers had been remarkably loyal and its sales performance through the recession had been better than that of many retailers and only marginally worse than the retailing norm. So talk of the concept being dated or no longer relevant was nonsense. It was, however, important that a continual flow of new product was available in the shops. Athena was part of the teenage culture and its appeal to the fashion-conscious young meant that it had to be in touch with the latest fad or trend. So any changes would need to be handled with particular sensitivity. Unfortunately, when senior management were removed, they were not replaced for more than six months and, as at Ryman, prices were reduced across the product range. The top management gap meant that the essential supply of fresh new product to the shops was disrupted, which hit sales. The price reductions, again as at Ryman, were on products where price was not the dominant factor. It did not matter that much whether a poster was £6.99 or £5.99; what really mattered was that the image on the poster was absolutely up-to-the-minute in fashion and design terms. So, the lower prices did not increase sales volumes but simply reduced profits and cash flow.

In addition to the dramatic deterioration in the trading performance of each of the three retail chains, there was also the cost of the consultants. It has been estimated that as much as £10 million was spent on consultants and new projects, most of which were abortive. It was not difficult to see where the £45 million rights issue money had gone.

I regard it as a sad and unnecessary end to a bold enterprise. Jim Clark, one of the trio of non-executive directors who helped bring about my departure, was later to remark to a mutual friend, 'Terry might have made his mistakes but he got some things right. His successor didn't get anything right.'

The underlying businesses will, of course, continue and the names will still be seen on the high streets. Within days of the appointment of the receivers, each business had been parcelled up and sold on to third parties. As is almost always the case in receiverships, the sums realised were only a fraction of the true worth to a new, sensible, long-term investor. Thorn-EMI, which purchased Dillons, seems to have struck a particularly good bargain. I wish them all well under their new owners; they will always have a very special place in my heart.

INDEX